GET SH*I DONE

THE GSD FACTOR

THE POWER OF BEING CONFIDENT AND IGNITING
YOUR PROFESSIONAL AND PERSONAL EMPOWERMENT

**MISHA
BLEYMAIER-FARRISH**

GSD

FACTOR™ PUBLISHING

The GSD Factor
Copyright © 2023 by Misha Bleymaier-Farrish

Published by
The GSD Factor Publishing
www.gsdfactor.com
info@gsdfactor.com
6688 Nolensville Road, Ste. 108-107
Brentwood, TN 37027-8833

Printed in the United States of America

A special thanks to the GSD Factor Publishing Team:
Book Coach + Editor-in-Chief: Qualia C. Hendrickson
Editor: Alacia Reynolds
Cover Design: Ella Carlton Shirk
Interior Design: Carla Green
Author Headshot: Mat Brown
Audio Book recorded at Dark Horse Recording in Franklin, Tennessee
Sound Engineer: Drew Boals

ISBN 979-8-9877272-0-1 (paperback)
ISBN 979-8-9877272-1-8 (ebook)
ISBN 979-8-9877272-2-5 (audiobook)

To my daughter:

May you use your voice to raise other voices.

May you stand on my shoulders and break glass ceilings.

May you run through the doors that I hope to break for you.

May you continue to be brave enough to be the solo girl on the

boys baseball team, and just sing loud your GSD Factor life.

TABLE OF CONTENTS

Introduction 1

ATTRIBUTE ONE:

Be Confident. 9

    This Is Me 11

    Your True Authentic Self 25

    Use Your Voice. 39

    Passion and Dedication 53

ATTRIBUTE TWO:

Be Inquisitive 65

    Always Learn Something 67

    Your Clan 83

    Your Insiders Board 95

    Hold with Open Hands 103

ATTRIBUTE THREE:

Be Imaginative 111

    Dream Big 113

    Never Be Satisfied 125

    Problems Lead to Solutions 131

ATTRIBUTE FOUR:

Be Present 143

   Keep Showing Up 145

   Progress, Not Perfection. 153

   Be Present. 163

   Pivot Decisions 173

ATTRIBUTE FIVE:

Be Resilient. 183

   Resilient Life 185

   Trust the Timing 197

   Perspective 207

ATTRIBUTE SIX:

Be Influential 217

   Leader by Example 219

   Challenging the Stereotypes 233

   Heroes + Sheroes + Mentors 241

The GSD Factor Life 253

To Those Who Have Helped Me GSD 255

Resources 257

INTRODUCTION

The day had come. December 31st, hours before the ball dropped to signify the coming new year. While everyone else in the country was down in the streets partying or in their homes celebrating with family, my team and I were adding the final touches to our audit. For six weeks, my team and I worked crazy hours under immense pressure and managed to complete one of the most complicated and intense financial audits our company had encountered. I'm talking about a massive information security overhaul. This type of project would normally take years to complete, and here we were barreling towards a six-week completion goal. I was accustomed to being called in to do the inconceivable, so this was nothing new for me. The crazy thing, though, is that my superiors, the people who should have been rooting for my success, seemed to be hoping for the opposite.

At this point in my career, I was on the brink. I had come off of maternity leave to find my job different than it had been before. For weeks, I could feel a hostility directed at me that I couldn't explain. I had returned to such an immense amount of work and pressure, that after a while, the only conclusion I could come to was that my company, a major insurance and financial services organization, was working to make me quit or have me fired, whichever came first. So, when at the end of the year, they assigned me this behemoth of a project, I knew that they all assumed I would fail.

It was, essentially, an impossible project, because the timeline was impractical. They assigned the project the week leading into Thanksgiving, and it was due New Year's Day. Six weeks. Six weeks to prepare for an audit for which *months* would have been an unreasonable timeline. There was no way it would happen, and they knew it. Additionally, because it was an audit that was so important to the organization, they knew that when it failed, they would have cause to fire me. They had handed me a ready-made fail project with the intent to make me the scapegoat.

What they didn't expect, however, was that I would use this as motivation. I am a master at getting shit done, or as I like to say, "GSDing." This project, though meant to destroy me, simply stirred a fire-in-the-belly passion to prove them wrong. This was dedication in action, and I was going to GSD the shit out of it.

For six weeks, I only took Thanksgiving Day and Christmas Day off. My vendor and fellow colleagues showed up. On Christmas Eve, we were working. On weekends, we were working. They knew what was at stake. They saw the injustice and said, "We run with you; just tell us how fast." That vendor and those colleagues are still dear friends today. And guess what? We delivered. We made the deadline. On New Years' Day, I submitted the completed audit with all corresponding documentation to the surprise of my managers. Not only did we meet all the expectations of the audit, that auditor said that it was the best run, best laid out, and most organized audit he had ever been through, and he had been through a lot over his 30-year career for a nationally and world recognized bank.

That experience, though challenging, is only one of many similar situations that I've faced in my life, situations that pushed me beyond my physical, emotional, and mental limits. Challenges like this have required me to pull from many different places to achieve success. In those moments, I channel the strength and ingenuity of my family and ancestors. I refer back to all the lessons my parents taught me, all the times I had been counted out because of gender, age, educational status, or physical impairments. All of these combined experiences ultimately made me who I am – a woman who knows how to get shit done – my life's motto.

Now, when I say "get shit done," I'm not trying to coin a catchphrase or hashtag. It's more than that. The GSD Factor is an attitude that helps you accomplish seemingly insurmountable feats. It's a mindset that helps you cultivate an unshakeable confidence in your identity and your abilities. It's practical execution. The GSD Factor requires activating tools in both your personal and professional life. I believe that every single one of us has the GSD Factor within us, but maybe, for some of you, it just hasn't been activated. Maybe your journey has caused you to experience things that have muted your GSD Factor drive or motivation. You've had some struggles and obstacles that have caused your confidence to waver, but the essence of the GSD Factor is still there. Do you consistently find yourself in situations where you feel like an "other" or an "only" because of gender, age, ethnicity, or simply because you march to the beat of your own drum? Maybe you're a dreamer who's constantly looking for ways to improve or questioning the status quo. If you inspire others with your resilience and ability to be fully present in all situations, or if you often feel drawn to lead and to use your voice to influence others, then the GSD Factor is for you.

Now that we've established the GSD Factor, here's a little about me. My name is Misha Bleymaier-Farrish. I'm an entrepreneur, founder, career coach, speaker, technology strategist, insurance expert, program management specialist, military-family member, non-profit organization board member, mentor, wife, and mother. I'm an advocate for the under-voiced, mentoring the next generation of business leaders across insurance and technology and equipping those that need professional direction and clarity. I'm also the Founder and CEO of a consulting firm that works with global clients across industries to provide expertise in innovative technology, business integration, and operational needs. As you can tell, I wear many hats. I've been blessed with many talents, and I honor those blessings by making sure I'm operating as efficiently, authentically, and purposefully as possible. I get shit done because I don't want to waste or squander the gifts that have been entrusted to me.

Anyone who knows me, knows that I love to dream big, question the status quo, and just GSD. My team would tell you I'm the GSD boss. My kids would tell you I'm the GSD Momma, which to them means "Get stuff done." Some have even said, about me: "There goes Misha, GSDing!"

Throughout my life, I've always been known as a person who could execute, under pressure or otherwise. I realized fairly early that my propensity to solve problems and find success in challenging situations didn't come so easily to everyone. Consequently, I constantly find myself meeting people and almost instantly being asked for advice with a difficult task or problem. My experiences birthed this GSD mindset, and the benefits of GSD living motivate me to share this concept with others.

I know what you're thinking: *What is the GSD Factor? Why do I need it, and how will having a GSD mindset help me in the future?*

There are six key attributes that come to mind when I think about living the GSD Factor life. It's a lifestyle and state of being, so in order to live out the GSD Factor, you must:

1. Be Confident
2. Be Inquisitive
3. Be Imaginative
4. Be Present
5. Be Resilient
6. Be Influential

Someone with an activated GSD Factor has the confidence to know their true, authentic self and their own voice and has the assertiveness to speak their truth and be heard. They have the humility to be inquisitive and know that they are not the smartest people in the room, but the ability to mobilize the right team and people to ensure that they are open to the fullness of life. They're imaginative and are not afraid to dream big. They're never satisfied with the status quo, and say, "I'm here. What can we improve? What is impossible that we can make possible?" They know to be present and trust the process even when it seems that there are more pivots than plans. They have the stamina, grit, and perseverance to acknowledge that life can be shit sometimes and the resilience to turn the negatives into positives. Finally, they have influence. They lead by example, look to the future, and bring the next generation of leaders along with them, propping them on their own shoulders. As you read through this book, other contributing attributes to the GSD Factor will surface and come to life before your eyes, but these six attributes are the foundational principles from which all other aspects of the GSD Factor develop. They are the attributes that I have cultivated throughout my lifetime and the ones that I find in common with other GSDers I've encountered along my journey.

Throughout this book, I share my stories, life lessons, and outlook on how to GSD. I've had to understand first-hand the opportunities and challenges that come from being a working parent in both the insurance industry and technology space. Both industries demand long days, sprints or enrollment seasons, overnight releases – you name it. I will discuss ways in which I've activated and grown my GSD Factor and how you can in your own life. If there is a particular attribute that resonates with you, sparking a desire for growth in that area, I've provided some prescriptive and practical steps.

Anyone who knows me or works with me knows that I like to summarize at the end of any meeting or email to make sure that we are all aligned and that our next actionable steps are clear. This is a gentle way to remind everyone of what was discussed and holds everyone accountable for the next steps to move things forward. Therefore, at the end of each chapter, I'll quickly provide some final thoughts and you'll also find optional assessments with actionable next steps to grow that attribute's muscle. Being armed with this knowledge and data will enable you to self-regulate and begin to become more efficient and confident in living your best GSD Factor life.

HOW TO READ THIS BOOK

Our daily lives and interactions provide opportunities to learn, and these life lessons or nuggets of information can rapidly change your life's trajectory.

Throughout this book, the GSD Factor attributes and the personal lessons from my life's experiences are woven into the chapters. My hope is that these stories will encourage and empower you to activate the GSD Factor within you. I'm not only a strong believer that you can learn something from any experience; I'm walking evidence that it's true. Whether it's your own experience or something you hear along the way that makes an impact, you can learn what to do and what not to do. But I also want to hear from you – my readers, my fellow GSDers.

There are questions or journal prompts at the end of each chapter. You can write your answers directly in the book or visit www.gsdfactor.com to join our GSD Factor Hub where you can digitally capture your answers. By joining, you will be instantly connected to me, my team, and a worldwide community of GSDers just like you. Each of us has a story to share. I want to hear yours!

Your GSD Clan wants to hear yours. I want to hear about the times in your life when you have embodied the GSD Factor, or, perhaps, you are experiencing some situations and obstacles and need some real-time encouragement and guidance on how to GSD. I'd love to hear about it. I'm a strong believer in individuals collaborating to empower and encourage one another as we trailblaze our industries and bring about much needed change.

You'll also find even more content for your NEW or RENEWED GSD Factor life throughout the GSD Factor Hub. We have created the GSD Factor Score and assessments for each of the six attributes that will provide prescriptive recommendations based on which areas you want to improve. My GSD Factor Podcast features conversations with leaders and experts in various fields and industries ranging from insurance and diversity and equality in the workplace, to technology and everything in between. If there is a topic that is relevant in the world today, we will cover it! Can't find something that resonates? Post to the community or message me directly. I also want to empower you to find other tools throughout your life as you hone in on, grow into, and progress through that attribute. Remember, we are looking to achieve progress not perfection.

At the end of this book, you'll also find a resources page, where I provide a list of inspiring people, innovating companies, and research that I've learned from, and which I mention throughout the book.

Through all your interactions with GSD Factor, my team and I want to help reignite the GSD Factor within you. We want to help you realize that you are the key to changing your outcomes. We want to help you jump start that new chapter or new career. Whatever your story is, we are ready to listen and encourage you along the way. Don't worry; we are with you every step of the way.

The biggest thing is to connect with other GSDers that are walking your same journey. Share and learn together; laugh and cry, and know you are not alone. I am grateful that you have chosen to embark on this journey with me. Let's stay connected, so we can collaborate to harness the power of teamwork, or as we like to say here: Let's GSD! Welcome to your GSD Factor life.

ATTRIBUTE ONE

BE **CONFIDENT**

The power and confidence in knowing your true
authentic self, knowing your voice, and speaking
your truth so that you are heard. You lead
by example with assertiveness, giving you a
sense of empowerment and confidence.

66

Authenticity is a collection of choices that we have to make every day. It's about the choice to show up and be real. The choice to be honest. The choice to let our true selves be seen.

—Brené Brown, *The Gifts of Imperfection*

99

THIS IS ME

The Frankfurt Book Fair is the largest book fair in the world. Held every year in mid-October, thousands of distributors, publishers, writers, multimedia and technology professionals, and, of course, booklovers, attend the week-long event to showcase their latest books, strategize for their upcoming year, preview new works, and network. All the major players in the international book business attend, and major deals for licensing and publishing rights are made. There are booths, presentations, speakers, workshops, and books as far as the eye can see. Basically, everybody who is anybody in the book business is there, so to say it is a big deal would be an understatement.

I must have been one of those major players because at the tender age of nine, I traveled with my dad to Frankfurt, Germany for this book fair. At the time, Dad was the vice president of international sales for books and music for a contemporary Christian publishing and music company. He attended the fair every year and was an incredible networker. Dad had the gift of gab and knew how to leverage it. He had a natural instinct for connecting with people, and he could easily spot that same gift in others. Dad would later tell me how he saw that ability to connect with people in me at an early age. There were times in my early years, according to

Dad, that I would stop complete strangers and ask them if I could pray for their "boo-boos." Instances like that showed him that I not only had a special concern for helping people, but I also had a confidence that emboldened me to talk to anyone. Looking back at it, I believe that he must have specifically taken me on this trip to ignite that confidence in me. Dad traveled two-thirds of the year, and as my sister and I got older, he had committed to taking us on some of his most favorite business trips. Even though this was my first and only time to attend the Frankfurt Book Fair with him, that experience definitely lit the spark that has been burning the fire of confidence and connection in me all these years later.

On this particular trip, he saw my sales and networking potential and decided to give me an opportunity to hone that skill set. He would later state that my enthusiasm and excitement was a magnet for people, so he put me in charge of the children's book section. My job was to read every new release that we were showcasing and be able tell people about it. Sounds pretty easy, right? Maybe for an adult who had years of training and experience in sales, but I was nine! So, for weeks, I read the books we would be showcasing, and Dad prepared me to sell.

These conferences are massive and extremely overwhelming because everyone is trying to sell something. There are about 7,000 different exhibits from over 100 different countries. In order to make a deal, vendors have to be unique, somewhat aggressive and, most importantly, confident. Somehow, I knew, at nine years old, that if I didn't put myself out there, I wouldn't make the connections that I needed. Dad knew that too, and he prepared me for how to engage people at an international conference. We prepared talking points on each book, just in case someone wanted to know about the author, topic, age group, etc. He taught me to make eye contact, smile, and then speak so that people would come into my booth and want to learn more. Dad also prepared me for rejection by telling me that it was a normal thing. He emphasized that

I would have to get through a "no" to get to a "yes," and I quickly realized that the faster you get through the "no," the better! I got to set up my first booth (and I assure you, it was not the last) and practiced my book elevator pitches. Then, I took a deep breath because it was show time. I was ready!

That day, I made my way around to the other booths, introducing myself and getting to know the neighbors. I talked about the books Dad brought and whatever else I could think of. Thankfully, I had my dad's gift of gab, so the conversation flowed freely. I don't remember any other children being there in a professional capacity, if you will, but nobody seemed to be surprised by my presence. I guess that meant I fit in pretty well. Looking back on the experience, I can see how I naturally realized the importance of connecting with people. It's not hard to find commonalities with people; it just takes effort. I wasn't afraid to make the effort, even at nine. I now know that this was one of those turning points in my life that proved that I was no ordinary nine-year-old. I was able to engage with people and navigate those interactions effortlessly. Even if I was faced with a no, I went back one more time to see if I could win them over. If I could, great! If I couldn't, it was okay because it was great interaction practice.

Fast forward to my present-day career, and we can see the impact this early experience had on me. I've never been afraid to go to conferences, talk to strangers, network, and identify ways my organization can assist them. My experience at the Frankfurt Book Fair is one of those memories that will stay with me for the rest of my life, and it is one of the moments that helped shape who I am professionally. Working at the book fair gave me an early glimpse of what I would later discover to be the Get Shit Done Factor, or GSD Factor for short. That nine-year old girl learned what it meant to be confident and comfortable in her own skin and how to leverage that confidence to connect with people. Dad saw a spark that, throughout the years, has kept the fire burning in me to accomplish my goals. The Frankfurt Book Fair is a constant reminder of where this mindset began. I couldn't put a name to it then, but I know now that this trip helped shape my assertiveness, dedication, and my voice. I tip my hat to my dad and thank him for those skill sets that he taught me at such a young age.

To really understand me, the GSD Factor, and why I believe so strongly in it, you have to know my family and the way I was raised. The GSD Factor isn't just one quality or trait, but it's a set of attributes that are common to people who have confidence, set trends, make changes, and lead with conviction. I come from a long line of GSDers. The Bleymaiers, my dad's side of the family, were natural-born innovators. My sister and I often joke about the Bleymaier trait when we hear about a family member making something out of nothing, being called to fix a problem, or creating a new way of doing something. We always say something like, "Oh, that's a Bleymaier thing," or "He/she's just being a Bleymaier." It's one of those "funny because it's true" jokes. My grandfather General Joseph S. Bleymaier, or Papa Joe as we called him, was a major general in the United States Air Force who fought in World War II and led Air Force support efforts for NASA in the race to the moon and the Titan rocket program. He was brilliant, a literal rocket scientist. My uncle Gene Bleymaier served as athletic director at Boise State University for thirty years where he spearheaded the decision to use their now-famous, blue turf and helped transform BSU football into the amazing program that it is today.

That's just the Bleymaiers. My mom's side of the family is also full of amazing people who accomplished great things. Vincent Williams, my maternal grandfather, started his trailblazing early. He mastered the organ as a boy and studied at the Royal Academy of Music, which is the oldest conservatory in the United Kingdom, one of the most prestigious music schools in the world, and alma mater of "The Rocket Man" himself, Sir Elton John. If that isn't enough, Papa also survived imprisonment at a Japanese prison camp during World War II with enough fortitude and forgiveness to later become an Anglican priest.

Finally, the two closest and most influential relatives who helped shape and mold me into the person I am today are my parents. My dad, Ted Bleymaier, was no stranger to setting trends and setting the standard for those around him. He excelled in athletics and played in two Rose Bowls at Stanford University. Professionally, he embodied the Bleymaier flare for innovation by starting the international music and publishing division for Maranatha Music and, later, Word Entertainment. At one point in his career, anybody in the international music and/or book publishing business had either been mentored or coached by my dad. He built a sophisticated and efficient network from nothing that would serve as the blueprint for international distribution in music and book publishing spaces for decades to come. My mom, who showed me how to be resilient and how to use my voice for good, left her whole family and moved across the world from Wales to California to start a new life. She had to learn the new customs and traditions of the United States all while navigating the challenges of being a working wife and mother – before the internet! This is the legacy I come from. Imagine what it must have been like for me to grow up and find my purpose knowing that the blood running through my veins stemmed from that kind of lineage. There's a certain pride and standard of excellence that my parents expected from me (and my sister) that shaped the ways in which I navigate life. They instilled the principles of the GSD Factor in me before I could even put a name to those qualities. I don't know what it's like to be average or do the bare minimum because Bleymaiers and Williamses are made of ingenuity, innovation, and excellence.

I knew at an early age that, like them, I was different. My family's history and my parents' expectations set me apart from the crowd, but I also had an innate drive and motivation to do things my own way. I wasn't interested in conforming to other people's views or expectations. I often asked lots of questions, even in the midst of getting answers such as, "You don't need to ask that," or "Why are you asking; you are a girl."

All throughout middle school and high school, I had multiple businesses. Dog sitting, house sitting, cleaning, organizing, you name it! At one point in high school, I had such a thriving dog-sitting business that I had to hire my sister and her friends as subcontractors to help out. I had always dreamed of becoming a professional dancer, and even though I faced some extreme, physical struggles that ultimately ended my dance career, I knew that whatever profession I pursued, I would not let the traditions, expectations, or limitations of the culture around me determine my path. I was keenly aware, even as a teenager, that this kind of thinking wasn't the norm, and it would challenge the ideologies of most people around me. As a senior in high school, there was a guy who wanted to ask me out, but when he learned of my career aspirations and lack of interest in immediately becoming a "Mrs.," he quickly ended things. I can still recall a conversation we had on the back of his truck when he asked, "Don't you want to get married and take on someone else's name?" to which I responded, "I do want to get married, at some point, but I won't be losing my maiden name. I will hyphenate." He replied, "Is that allowed?"

Sidenote: I guess it is, because here I am, years later, a happily married woman, mother, multiple business owner, and author with a hyphenated last name!

Post high school was a nontypical journey. Injuries and ailments began to thwart my progress as a professional dancer, so I chose to work around my limitations by co-founding a thriving dance school while starting my career in the business world, straight out of high school. I even began taking some college courses online, until I suffered a major injury while dancing. The next five years would include four knee surgeries, loss of my dance school dream, a decrease in seeing the need for college, and a drive to keep working in corporate America, learning all that I could.

As you can imagine, being a woman in business with no college degree but with a shit ton of life experience was a new one for the corporate world. My entry into corporate America, working for a company that manufactured collectible items, stationery, and small gifts was like a crash course in Business 101. Looking back on it, it seems like I worked in every department and did every job possible, from accounts receivable and project management to putting labels on boxes for shipping. I did it all. That job served as a training ground for me and was excellent preparation for the career ahead. However, I did not have a college degree, and because of my unorthodox way of entering the business world, I had to rely on a recruiter to be my voice, be my advocate, and pave the way for my next career move. Boy, was I blessed with the best business Fairy Godmother. She coached me, mentored me, and was my talking cover letter. I will be forever grateful to her. She showed up for me, and she didn't even know me.

The next position I landed, with the help of my recruiter, was in sales and marketing for an organization in the insurance and financial space. These arenas were historically male-dominated industries, but that didn't scare me. I was often told that I was too bossy or too confident. My favorite comment was, "Your reputation precedes you and not in a good way." When I asked why, my boss told me it was because if I was asked to join a project, call or meeting, something had to be fixed; the project or audit was behind and needed to get back on track; or the impossible needed to be made possible, which made people feel uncomfortable. I also heard, "That's not how women act in corporate" a lot. This was said to me by both men and women alike. What was more astonishing to me was that in the twenty-first century ideologies like this were, and still are, a thing. It's hard to believe that people still hold these stereotypes of women. Little did I know that my career path would take me into technology, which is even worse than typical corporate America in some cases, but, again, I am here for the journey. I am here to show up. If this is what my destiny has prepared, then so be it.

The frequency of these comments and stories throughout my life placed me at a crossroads many times. I often had to ask myself: should I change myself, my personality, my skills, even when I know that this is my true, authentic self, or do I adapt and conform? I knew that I was not the typical businesswoman. I am a Type A personality, highly organized, who can get a lot of shit done by springing into immediate action. People were often shocked that this southerner could curse and talk fast without a southern accent, and I was often compared to a New Yorker with my approach to business. I thrive on creating plans to solve chaotic situations. I have mobilized incredible teams to make the impossible possible for over twenty years in operations and technology. This is me. This is who I am. I come from generations on both sides of my family that just got shit done. Should I change me because I don't fit the typical model, or do I remain steadfast, fully embracing my true authentic self?

You can guess which path I chose. It hasn't always been the easiest. In fact, there are not many easy days because there are negative stereotypes, perceptions, and opinions that fly in my face on a daily basis, even to this day, but this hasn't stopped me. Many times, I have been the solo girl on the tech team or the solo woman in the boardroom, but what I've experienced is that my colleagues, partners, and clients know they are always getting the true me, which has fostered deep trust and fierce loyalty from them over the years. Still, even today I face these struggles. Recently, I was having a branding conversation with a nationally-acclaimed marketing agency, and they told me my name was too difficult, definitely too long, not spellable, not memorable, and people would never find me, therefore creating a branding nightmare.

In order to gain more insight into entrepreneurship, I signed up for Nicole Walters' $1K1Day life coaching course. Of course, the topic of brand, name, and URL was one of the first things we tackled, and one of the first things that she and her team said to us was, "The world learned how to say and spell Oprah; they will learn your name, and they will learn how to spell it." My website, www.mishableymaierfarrish.com, was born just after that!

Now, times are changing but at an extremely slow pace, and there is still room for improvement. Women continue to break glass ceilings, and there are still many "first woman in history to..." moments that my young daughter and I are witnessing firsthand. Let's take, as an example, one of my favorite whiskeys, Uncle Nearest. In 2021, they were the first and only major spirit brand to have an all-female executive team and be the most awarded female-owned spirit brand in American history. It was built by and continues to be led by a leadership team of all women. The company is fifty percent female with one-hundred percent pay equity. Well done, Uncle Nearest! On this front, I am pleased that we are watching history unfold, but there's still much progress and work to be done.

Though Uncle Nearest is changing the game with its woman-led executive team, much of corporate America is still lagging far behind in gender equality, especially regarding women in leadership. Even today, as a woman-owned business with multiple companies, men tend not to respond to my emails, but rather my male business partner's. It's astonishing to both of us. Both he and my husband are pro-female in the workforce and have supported their wives' careers. My partner is always quick to respond and remind them that I'm the founder and sign both the contracts and issue the payments. I laugh and let it go, but it's unfortunate that it's still a thing.

Now, in certain areas of the United States and throughout the world there are expectations projected onto women and their choices around family and career. For example, growing up in the south, I was aware of the expectation that women take on their spouse's last name, that women should be married by a certain age, have children and devote their lives to what others think they should be.

As I moved from organization to organization and continued to rise up the ranks, I kept being confronted with negatively-intended comments that I chose to turn into positives. I was constantly dismissing projections of what my life was supposed to look like through other people's eyes. Those in my personal life would wonder, "How can she be in her twenties and not be dating or married? Why can't she see that she is already too old to be a wife and mother?" In my professional life, the questions were often, "How can she be so young, successful, and female?" Despite all that, I just kept being me. I kept showing up. I kept living because, after all, I had been given a second chance (more to come later in the book about this second chance). I knew and trusted that God had a plan, and He didn't give me these dreams for no reason. I continued to be a trailblazer.

One of the main reasons I work so hard to blaze trails professionally is because of the two tiny humans who look up to me personally. In addition to being a GSD Factor professional, I am also a GSD Factor mother to a daughter and a son. My daughter is a mini-me with lots of interests in sports, music, drama, and STEM. Her future may be in the STEM world, which means that there are tons of opportunities for her to hold the title of "first woman" to do something. Because of this, my husband and I have raised her with a strong voice, the space to know who she is, and encouraged her to be confident, bold and, many times, courageous. We have instilled this into both our kids at early ages, but our daughter is likely to face more challenges because of her gender. My son is the youngest of the two and is still enjoying life and social interactions in their purest, most innocent forms. My daughter, however, is a little older, and since we have taught her to be unapologetically authentic, she has already faced some negative responses to her boldness. She has the Bleymaier trendsetter trait, and her proclivity to choose her own path rather than following the crowd is probably strange to most children. I get it. Most adults aren't accustomed to that either. As her parents, it is our job to prepare her for the hurtful things that people may say, and unfortunately, we have had to endure some of this negativity with her.

Kevin Hart, comedian, and actor, often says, "You do you, boo boo!" I love that statement because it encourages people to focus on their own actions and behaviors, instead of judging or ridiculing others. That's where the GSD Factor mindset begins. It starts with confidence, a firm knowledge of self, and for me, that means remembering that little girl at the Frankfurt Book Fair. It's every story and memory I have of family members who have made history by being the first or the best at something. It's the years of obstacles and trials that would have broken others, but somehow made me stronger and better. This is who I am. I have lived the GSD Factor my entire life. I am now raising the GSD Factor next generation, and through this book, I hope to share with you my continued journey into being a GSDer. Will you join me?

GSD moment of reflection

Answer these prompts in the space below or on the GSD Factor Hub:

Fill out this sentence. My name is _____ ,

and I'm a _____ . I'm proud of my _____

skill sets. They set me apart because they show how

_____ I am.

What advice would you give your younger self?

_____

_____

_____

What would you hope your older self has accomplished in 10 years?

_____

_____

_____

www.gsdfactor.com

A SPACE TO DREAM BIG . . .

A SPACE TO DREAM BIG . . .

YOUR TRUE AUTHENTIC SELF

You are a unicorn. This is one of the fundamental points to remember when we start to think about what the GSD Factor is. What does this mean? Why a unicorn?

I'm a mom to two great kids, and my husband and I are always looking for books and tools that can help them and us as we navigate this crazy thing of parenting in this day and age. One of our most favorite tools is called Slumberkins, an organization dedicated to helping families raise caring, confident, and resilient children through affirmations, stories, and creature characters. Slumberkins have developed these amazing characters and turned them into stuffed animals with beautifully-written stories meant to encourage children's emotional growth. Their story of the unicorn is one that shows tiny humans the power of authenticity, and it promotes this alongside bravery and friendship. The story's protagonist is the unicorn, who is unique and authentic but wants to fit in so badly with her new friends, the zebras. Throughout the story, she changes her look and the way she acts in a desperate attempt to conform to her peers. She misses the fact that she is losing herself in the process. She doesn't realize that what makes her unique is tied to her identity. It's her true, authentic self. This story is a creative way to teach kids confidence and self-acceptance, but the lesson is universal across all ages. The first GSD Factor attribute of being confident is directly related to this idea of the unicorn and embracing authenticity. Being confident and assertive about who you are and your beliefs is the fuel that propels one to action. GSDers celebrate uniqueness because we understand that differences cultivate stronger teams, families, and organizations. Diversity creates an atmosphere for endless possibilities, so being a unicorn – distinct, authentic, irreplicable – is an asset and a telltale sign of a person who gets shit done.

So many times, we find ourselves conforming to those around us. We change our look because that's what the celebrities and socials tell us to do. We change how we speak and what we say because it's what everyone else is doing or has done. We make ourselves smaller, so we can blend with the crowd. How much more interesting would life be if instead of changing our looks, personalities, and voices to fit in, we amplified the unique aspects of ourselves to enhance and enrich those around us? If we embraced being the unicorn? What if we used our peculiarities to tell a different story, a unicorn story, a GSD Factor story? Sure, our voice can still be heard in a choir, but when we step forward, into the spotlight, looking, sounding and acting a little differently, our voice is not only heard but remembered.

Let's apply this idea to our adult lives. I can speak directly to the need to embrace individuality and authenticity because I've had to implement that ideology in almost every aspect of my life, especially professionally. I detailed a little bit of my experiences with breaking into the tech and insurance space, but let me set the scene for you a little bit more. As a child, my dreams were to become a professional dancer. I never had any desire to work in corporate America, but my father always stressed the importance of having a back-up plan. I'm grateful for his wisdom in that area because as life would have it, health issues thwarted my plans for dance, proving my dad's point about the need for a plan B.

I began working at a company directly out of high school that gave me immediate, real-life experience in the business world. I was getting on-the-job training in many different areas of business administration – accounts receivable, customer service, project management, etc. The problem, however, was that when I began to look for professional advancement, I had to do so without having any formal education or certification to help me gain entry at a time when organizations were almost singularly focused on whether an applicant had a college degree. Now, if you look at my situation as an obstacle or a liability, like most organizations of the time, let me challenge you to see it as an opportunity. That's what the GSD Factor would encourage. Did I have the degree? No. Did I have transferable skills and experience? Absolutely. I was different, and my lack of a college degree didn't make me more or less valuable to the company. It just made me unique.

Over the years, I have learned to be confident and assertive about my learned experiences and proud of the distinct way in which I achieved success. I have been able to leverage my story and my background to work my way up to positions of leadership fairly quickly. I also believe that my unique career trajectory has made me more adept at recognizing transferable skills in potential hires, which has been a major contributor to my success in building sustainable and effective teams. It is the embracing of my authenticity that has allowed me to move with confidence throughout my career. I recognize that I am a unicorn in this industry. I celebrate that, and I desire to help others do the same.

We all have unique skills and attributes that we can bring to the table. The challenge is figuring out how to make those skills evident to potential employers, clients or customers. Does your LinkedIn profile look like everyone else's? Could your picture be one of you laughing versus standing stoic? Maybe you can use a background of a city instead of the white backdrop in your picture. What does your overview say about you? Does your personality shine through?

One time, a new contact reached out to me and said, "Your profile introduction is stellar and inspiring! Can we connect?" My profile looks a little different. The standard LinkedIn profile is a brief description of a person's job title. Mine is "GSD – Get Shit Done." That sparks conversation. It makes me stand out. People remember it; it sparks their curiosity, and they want to talk to me. What about you? Does your summary, profile overview, or cover letter do that? Do you get messages from random people saying, "You inspired me" by your profile introduction? Consider making a few changes to set yourself apart from the crowd. It doesn't have to be drastic or jarring. Just remember, people don't forget unicorns.

When you write your cover letter, does it follow the traditional format? Why not change it up? Here is an example of a cover letter that has gotten me more responses than not:

Are you looking for a team member with a diverse background in Sales, Marketing, Operations, and Technology? Perhaps someone that can understand the needs of the organization up and down the corporate ladder, whether it's communicating project plans with the IT group or strategically collaborating with the C level on the roadmap for growth?

Hello, I'm Misha Bleymaier-Farrish, and I would appreciate the opportunity to connect with you to discuss partnering together to see how we can dream big and execute with excellence to make <insert company here> the next trailblazer in the industry.

You can learn more about my company here and feel free to connect with me on LinkedIn.

The number one thing responders say when they reach out to me after reading that cover letter is, "It stood out; it was different." That's being a unicorn. That's exercising your GSD Factor.

Anna Wintour, Editor-In-Chief of *Vogue Magazine* and one of the most iconic figures in the fashion world, is a great example of someone who confidently embraces her authenticity and uniqueness. I was inspired by her teaser video for *Masterclass,* a series of online classes taught by some of the most talented, respected, and acclaimed leaders, thinkers, artists, and innovators in the world. She talks about all the things she will teach and cover in her course, her accomplishments and achievements. She mentions some of her experiences, both good and bad. Then at the end says, "I'm Anna Wintour, and this is my Masterclass." I just love that! How many times do we say our names first and then launch into our roles, experiences, etc.?

I figured out, pretty early in my career, that in order to make a lasting impression, I needed to make sure I was different, even down to the way I meet people. I don't just launch straight into a verbal resume-review with people. I focus more on asking them questions and finding commonalities. I truly listen to people and show them that I am interested in who they are and not just what they can do for me. People remember genuine connections, so when we finally do reconnect, it feels authentic and mutually beneficial.

If you are a child of the eighties and raised by business parents, you were taught the importance of the business card or the leave behind. We all had one! Shit, I had one in high school! However, in my twenties, I started thinking, "What happens to a business card? Most of the time it gets thrown away, right?" Consequently, I stopped printing them. Instead, when I began interacting with a new contact or a new prospect, and we came to the point of exchanging business cards, I started saying, "Give me your phone, and I'll insert my contact information into your phone, send a quick text and reply. That way we are already locked in." At first, people looked at me as if I had ten heads, but once I started getting into a rhythm, it became so natural that people just went with it. It was different. It was thinking outside the box. Never mind that, it was a time and cost saver. It was the unicorn move!

When we introduce ourselves to someone, how many times do we start with normal chit chat and then move into the true questions? What if you were to answer a question with a question? What if you were to list off a unique skill set of yours or a unique experience? What if you changed things up in how you interacted with people and the world? Whether it's your email communications or in person interaction, you would leave an impression. After attending conferences where 5K-250K people attend your interaction with that person will stay with them far beyond leaving the conference.

Given my family legacy, especially in the military and space expeditions, you will hear lots of references to the Bleymaier favorite movie, *Apollo 13*. This movie, directed by Ron Howard, is a dramatization of the events that surrounded the technical difficulties of NASA's 1971 lunar-landing mission. It is a story of courage, quick-thinking and composure under life-threatening pressure. One of my favorite scenes is where Gene Kranz, the chief flight director played by Ed Harris, has just called a meeting, and he is trying to understand the capabilities of the systems they have. He says to the team: "I don't care about what anything was DESIGNED to do, I care about what it CAN do." Harris's character dared to challenge the status quo and push the team to think outside of the box. It was that kind of thinking that helped the team to solve the problem, ultimately bringing the stranded astronauts back to earth safely. If you ever find yourself up against what seems like an impossible situation, and something is stirring you to try a different solution or present a unique viewpoint, go for it. It might seem like a long-shot, but be confident that your knowledge and experience have prepared you for such a time as this. That's a unicorn! That's the GSD Factor in action!

Someone without the GSD Factor attitude would have just accepted that the rocket and the lunar module were designed to do this specific thing and this specific thing alone. They would have written the cover letter, copied the profile or practiced the same introduction speech exactly the way that everyone has done it. Perhaps you are presenting to the executive team or board, and you feel like your slides and talking points have to follow the exact format. Let me tell you, friend, even if the slide is cookie cutter across all the presenters, the story that accompanies it does not have to be that. Your uniqueness, your storytelling ability, and your voice CAN shine through! You can absolutely do it!

If you're a corporation, embracing uniqueness and being willing to be a unicorn can have enormous benefits. Let's apply this mindset to a real-life business scenario, such as a process or a technology stack.

Most IT staff are focused on the manual or training, which tells you what the technology or application was designed to do. This isn't necessarily a bad way of thinking, and it's pretty common to the technology space. What if you were to look through a different lens, though? So many companies today say that their process has to have X amount of steps. Why? Why that many steps? Could there be more, or could there be less? What if you could take what's existing and transform it to do something new, something different? How would that impact your team, your organization, and/or your individual contribution to your specific industry?

When I was young in my career and moving up the ranks quickly, it was because I embraced being a unicorn. I was constantly thinking outside the box because I wasn't intimidated or moved by the fact that my ideas didn't conform to the majority's thoughts or opinions. I made it a point to approach things differently and think about how things can be transformed. I have never been afraid of being the first one or the only one. Sure, it's a little unsettling to be the first to do or say anything. What if I'm rejected? What if people think I'm stupid? What if they laugh? Who cares?

At one point in my career, I worked for an organization that had a traditional process for getting important documents signed. This organization's main focus was supporting companies in the areas of insurance, data services, direct marketing, program administration and servicing. Like most companies, we would send letters by mail or courier, or even, the fax machine. One day back in 2008, I stumbled across DocuSign, a company that created a way for companies to manage and sign documents electronically. I proposed it to my leadership as the next big move in getting clients to sign from anywhere. No longer would we be paying travel expenses for the sales team to get a signature. No longer would we have to struggle reading illegible or incomplete faxes. No longer would we have to wonder, "Did they get it? Did they review, and did they sign?" DocuSign would be a game-changer because it would save us time and money. DocuSign was quicker and less expensive than the traditional travel or faxing for signatures, and it was safer, because it was all encrypted. It was the new thing. It was bold and brave.

When I discovered DocuSign, it was relatively new, and no one in our industry had embarked or taken the risk. I could feel that this was where technology and industry best practices were going, though. Unfortunately, my company didn't agree with my vision for DocuSign. Even after they rejected my proposal, I kept close tabs on DocuSign's success and continued to bring it up to the business. I continued to be shut down, until a decade later. You read that correctly. A full ten years went by, and, finally, that same organization said, "Let's do it. We are ready." FINALLY! Now were they a unicorn? No. Did they trailblaze the industry? No. Did they follow only when it wasn't right NOT to be using DocuSign? Yes. That's exactly what they did.

Friend, company: don't be that person or organization! DocuSign has become an industry staple now, but it wasn't back then. My employer could have saved a significant amount of money, time, and resources by taking a chance on it, but they didn't. They chose to be like the other zebras from the Slumberkins story. Don't do that! If you want to be the unicorn in your space, if you want to encompass the GSD Factor, do the thing that no one else is doing. Do the thing that your fellow zebras look at you and say, "That's crazy." That probably means it's the right thing. Be the unicorn! Be brave. Be bold. Be memorable. Be unique and be confident in your uniqueness!

Being a unicorn matters in your personal life too. When my daughter was in the first grade, she was assigned one of her first presentations for which she had to make a creative project and prepare a speech about her culture. The same way my father once helped me prepare for my presentations at the Frankfurt Book Fair, my husband and I worked with her, preparing, planning, selecting the creative elements she wanted to display and then the talking points of her speech. We knew it was going to be different from most kids' presentations, but she was excited. She practiced and even sent a video to all the family for the sneak peek. It turned out, though, that she ended up being one of the last kids to present in a class of twenty. Consequently, my daughter found herself being self-conscious about the fact that everyone else's presentations sounded the same across her class. She was embarrassed that hers was different. You can imagine that as a first grader being raised by a storytelling, technology mom, a data-analytics, storytelling dad, and a family with a long line of storytellers in all their professions, her presentation was different. She had a story to tell. As the other kids went through their presentations, she got scared. She was embarrassed. She so desperately wanted to fit in with the rest of her classmates. She wanted just to be one of the other kids.

When she stood up, she changed her entire speech and made it conform to what everyone else had done. She thought it would make her feel good afterwards. She thought my husband and I would be happy afterwards. She thought she would be proud of her effort, but instead she was sad. She was disappointed in her effort. We were disappointed because we knew all the time and preparation she had put in to put her mark on it. We knew that her presentation would likely be different from everyone else's because, after all, she has GSD Factor parents. She got in the car at pickup and started crying, fully aware that she had acted like a zebra and not like the unicorn that she is. She knew what being a unicorn looked like. She had been empowered and trained on how a unicorn acts and presents, but in the moment, she executed as a zebra. At that moment she felt what it's like not to be true to yourself, not to walk in the unicorn or GSD Factor way.

Here's what's most impressive about my daughter's experience. She knew that she had not lived up to her uniqueness, so she decided to correct her errors. The next day, our daughter let her teacher know that she was not content with her presentation. She told the teacher that she had practiced the presentation differently, and she asked if she could redo it at the end of class, if time permitted. Thankfully, there was extra time, and the teacher allowed my little unicorn to present. And present she did! She came home beaming with pride and excitement, not just because of the warm reception from both the teacher and her classmates after she presented, but because of the feeling of accomplishment and peace she got from being authentic. She shed those zebra stripes and reminded me of how important it is to honor my own authenticity at all times.

The question I have for you is this: Are you a unicorn or are you a zebra? Being a unicorn embodies the GSD Factor and builds that muscle of confidence each time you choose to stand boldly in your true, authentic self. Being confident becomes much easier when you are consistently embracing all of the differences and unique qualities that make you who you are. It's 'simple. The more you show up as your true self, the more assertive you can be in challenging and difficult situations.

Being a unicorn, being confident in your differences, says, "I'm here! Hear me! See me! My way may not be popular, but it will be memorable. You will know me. You will remember me." Being confident is the ability to stand unmoved in your identity. It is knowing your voice and speaking your truth so that you are heard. It's not letting others' expectations of who you are or what role they think you should take influence your life. Be confident in who you are, and don't diminish yourself to make others comfortable. This is your life, and the more you embrace your uniqueness, the more empowered you will feel and become. That's when you can really start to get shit done!

GSD moment of reflection

Answer these prompts in the space below or on the GSD Factor Hub:

What makes you a unicorn?

_____

_____

_____

How can you bring that into a problem you've been facing in your life? Could you use a different approach or perspective?

_____

_____

_____

What situation have you been evaluating solely from what something is designed to do vs what it can do?

_____

_____

_____

A SPACE TO DREAM BIG . . .

A SPACE TO DREAM BIG . . .

USE YOUR VOICE

If anyone knows my family, they know that we are passionate about fundraising. I'm not sure what motivated us more, sharing the story or reaching a goal, but we started fundraising at an early age. I mean in elementary school. My sister and I were both a part of the traveling swim team. Because this wasn't a school-supported sport, there were expenses associated with being on the team that athletes were responsible for covering. So, each year, the swim team would have fundraisers to help cover these expenses. Depending on the time of year, our campaign could have been Little Caesars frozen pizzas, Swan's frozen cookie dough, or wrapping paper. My sister and I were a team, and we were good! If we entered a fundraising competition, the athleticism in us had to make it a competition. We would win hands down. Our dad would sit down with us and strategize our goals, daily targets, and how many houses/families we needed to talk to as we were about to hit the streets! After our strategy sessions, we would role play and practice. Of course, being the oldest, I was tasked with handling most of the no or thanks but no thanks while my sister handled most of the yes customers.

Just like the Frankfurt Book Fair, Dad coached us on how to respond in every situation. When we would make a sale, we would leave the new customer with the next steps for their order, including details about when we would deliver. We even wrote out individual thank you notes for each donor. Yes! My sister was as young as eight, and I was twelve! Our dad would drop us off at one end of the subdivision and tell us where he expected us to be in the neighborhood by a certain time. The Bleymaier sisters were a force to be reckoned with! We were raising anywhere from $1,000.00-$1,500.00 on every fundraiser. That was a lot of money for two kids to raise in the 1990s. It drove our teammates crazy! We had gotten so good that one year, one of the parents simply wrote a check for his son because he suspected that the Bleymaier sisters would win the competition again. That didn't faze us or our dad, though. If anything, it just gave Dad another opportunity to show us how to use our voice to speak out against unfair treatment. He went right to the fundraising committee and petitioned for the creation of another award for the highest number of unique donors to make the competition fair again. We worked hard and earned the right to win those competitions, and our dad spoke up to make sure that the athletes who worked the hardest were rewarded for their efforts. In all honesty, we won the competition a number of times, but I suspect that my dad would've spoken up, even if we were not consistently winning because at his core, he was a person who wasn't afraid to advocate for those who could not.

Another major lesson about using our voice that I reflect on the most when remembering these fundraisers is how Dad made sure that we told our potential donors why we were raising money and what made it relevant to us. After my dad retired from the music and book publishing industry, he began working for non-profit organizations in the fundraising sector. He and my mom ran fundraising golf tournaments for organizations such as Habitat for Humanity, Young Life, and the Kidney Foundation. Their biggest focus was to tell the story and to make an emotional connection. In doing so, the hope was not only to secure a donation, but also to inspire the donor to share the story tenfold, ultimately amplifying the cause on a greater scale. Dad knew that sharing stories would create more empathy from potential donors and motivate them to give. Additionally, if the story really resonated with the donors, they would be more likely to share those stories with others and subsequently help spread awareness about whatever particular cause the organization was championing. Over his fourteen year career in nonprofit fund-raising, Dad helped to raise over $10M. Watching my parents use their voices to raise funds for these organizations gave me a front-row seat to see how impactful we can be when we use our voices and influence to advocate for good.

When Dad was diagnosed with Amyotrophic Lateral Sclerosis, also known as ALS or Lou Gehrig's Disease in 2012, there were no treatment protocols. ALS is a motor-neuron disease that gradually decreases the brain's ability to communicate with the body's muscles, eventually resulting in the inability to walk, talk, eat, and eventually breathe. Like most diagnosed with this disease, my dad was given a two-to-five-year life sentence and then told there was not a single treatment out there. The doctors just told him to go home and endure his final years as best he could. Now, anyone that knew my dad would agree that he never backed down from a challenge, an opportunity to share a story, or his latest favorite book, and this was no different. He took his diagnosis and said "OK." Mom and Dad were determined to network, share our story, and raise awareness and money to help others suffering from ALS. At the time, research was limited, and visibility was an important milestone. You name it, our family did it. Over the course of those two quick years, Dad read the Lou Gehrig speech at baseball games, became the chairman of the Nashville ALS walk, and flew all over the United States with other PALS (person with ALS), up until one month before he passed in April of 2014. Just a couple months later, the ALS ice bucket challenge would become a worldwide viral sensation that raised $135 million dollars. Dad would have been so proud of this amazing accomplishment of millions knowing about ALS and raising much needed funds for research and to support those suffering.

Over the years, fundraising taught me many lessons. It boosted my confidence in my ability to connect with people and have meaningful conversations. Most importantly, it showed me the power of my voice and the potential it has to reach the multitude. Your network may be small, but you never know how it can amplify. You may only tell one person, but it may be the RIGHT one person. Sometimes when we use our voice, even to the few people around us, it can have a snowball effect that can reach millions around the world.

A few years ago, my daughter came home from her first karate lesson and was so excited because she learned from her sensei that her voice is her strongest weapon. To hear, at the age of four, that her voice was her strongest weapon was a day of empowerment for her that she hadn't experienced before. She truly felt like Wonder Woman, Spider-Woman, and Batwoman all wrapped into one. She felt unstoppable. Now that will stay with her for the rest of her life.

In a perfect world, there would be no need for fundraising, and every struggle, disease, and cause would have the support that it needed. There would be no need for my daughter's sensei to start teaching his classes about the power in their voices. People would not need to stand in the gap and advocate for the underserved and under-voiced, because in a perfect world, people would not harm each other. However, we don't live in a perfect world.

Unfortunately, in this day and age, the use of our voice through certain platforms has become both positive and negative, with a heavy focus on the latter. The question is, what does this do for our mental health? History tells us that the lack of using our voices for good has been detrimental to individuals' outlooks on their personal and professional lives.

Research shows us that positive words can actually change one's brain and restructure it. Let's ponder this for a moment. If positive words can change one's brain structure, is it safe to assume that negative words, reinforced over and over again, are actually changing our brain waves as well? We aren't living in the most positive time, and I, wholeheartedly, believe we have restructured our brains. The impact this is having on governments, responses to pandemics, wars, etc. is troubling. We have been feeding our brains and the universe with negative energy. We have to stop. But how do we do that?

Let's look at this in our world today. We deserve to live in positivity, but it's not something that has an instant fix. It has to start with you and me speaking more positively within our personal and professional lives and the community around us. Our children deserve to grow up in a world where positivity is more the norm, especially because everyone isn't vibrating at the same level of positivity and kindness. There are people who, for whatever reasons, valid or not, live in a perpetual state of darkness and negativity.

When we're kids, we knew these people as bullies. My daughter, at the ripe old age of seven, was targeted by a fellow classmate and bullied both verbally and, eventually, physically. As a mother of a daughter who has experienced the verbal, emotional, and physical stresses of being the target of a bully, I want to ensure that she is ready and trained in the art of verbal warfare. Our voice is our strongest weapon, and we should use it. We should use it for good. Use it to build up. Use it in innovation, ideas, and exploration.

For you parents of bullies, out there, you have a choice. You can do something. You can get your child and family the help that they need, so that they can turn their lives around. They can be impacting the world for good and not for harm.

However, bullying is not just an adolescent struggle. There are grown, adult bullies in our workplaces, leading, teaching. You name it. If you are not speaking life, hope, and encouragement, you need to reconsider what you are saying. If you make fun of someone's clothes or hair, you are a bully. If you question their life choices, which is exactly that, a life choice, you are a bully. If you believe yourself superior to everyone else and that you are protected and absolved, you are a bully. As adults, we warn against being these types of people by saying: "Don't be a _____ ." Some of you inserted "bitch." Or maybe, "an ass." Whatever word you prefer to use to describe someone who uses words and actions to negatively impact others, you can apply it here.

I think we can all agree, at this point, that whoever coined the saying, "Sticks and stones may break my bones, but words will never hurt me" was a liar! Words do hurt, and if you've spent any time in the workforce, you can attest to the fact that people can say some hurtful things to and about you at work. I have had negative experiences with both men and women in professional environments who have used their voices to tear others down. What has been interesting in my experience is that the women were often much more hurtful to each other. Maybe, I'm the only one who noticed that, but my time in the corporate world showed me that the negative and unkind things said to women seemed more likely to be said by a woman than a man. Men say nasty things too, but ladies, your words cut deeper and sting more.

I had one colleague that was amazing at her role. She could command a Zoom conference call or a room and mobilize international C levels. She embodied the GSD Factor lifestyle. The men she worked with respected her role, her voice, her decisions and delivered. Her boss, however, was a woman that suffered from imposter syndrome, and she was jealous. She began to micro-manage her day, questioning the actions that were delivering results. This boss publicly humiliated my colleague and shamed her in front of others to the point that my colleague was starting to have negative physical manifestations from the verbal and emotional abuse. My colleague's boss, obviously, did not honor the power that her voice held in that role. She had an opportunity to speak words of affirmation and encouragement that would ultimately serve as an example for how women should be treated in the workplace. Her actions, unfortunately, represented the complete opposite and may have caused impressionable onlookers to believe this type of behavior was acceptable, since it was coming from a person in leadership who was also a woman. As a result, this high performing GSDer left that company to find opportunities elsewhere.

Some of the most surprising and most hurtful experiences I've had with women co-workers inappropriately using their voices happened during one of my pregnancies. I'm not sure what was in the water during that time, but my colleagues made it uncomfortable for me. I was accustomed to the off-color jokes about how much weight I would gain, how much I was eating, and how tired I was. Most of those comments came from men. The women, however, seemed to go out of their way to harass me about when and if I was coming back to work after giving birth, whether I would breast-feed or not, and making sure I completed all of my work before taking maternity leave. One particularly offensive moment happened after I returned from maternity leave. A female co-worker reported me to Human Resources because I kept my breast milk in the refrigerator. According to that co-worker, no one wanted to see my breast milk. As a result, Human Resources mandated that if I were to keep my milk in the refrigerator, I would have to make sure it was in a container that no one could see through. Imagine coming back from maternity leave after a traumatic birth experience and having to deal with petty complaints about the kind of container that held your breast milk.

Let's think about how that co-worker chose to use her voice in that instance. Instead of having a modicum of compassion for a fellow teammate and mother and using her voice to encourage and welcome me back to the team, she chose to use it to make a trivial complaint about a natural part of life. Ladies, I know we already have a great deal of pressure and expectations to live up to in the corporate world, but please be aware of how you are using your voices on the job, especially when it comes to your conversations with and about other women. It is easy for your own insecurities to shine through when you are managing or speaking to other ladies. Part of living out the GSD Factor, as a woman, is to make sure that you are using your voice to advocate and encourage other women, not to tear them down.

When women negatively speak into another woman's life, the ripple effects are much more career-damaging and crippling than what you do towards your male colleagues. According to research by Gender Equality Funds, "Women comprise 47% of the work-force, but only 4.8% of S&P 500 companies have female CEOs. Men are promoted at 30% higher rates than women during their early career stages. Women are paid 79 cents on the dollar of their male colleagues, and it's even worse for women of color. Fifty percent of women in STEM fields eventually leave their job because of hostile work environments." Women are already working against systemic inequalities that make it more challenging for them to succeed in the workforce, so we definitely don't need to add negative inter-actions with other women to the list.

I know there are some women leaders who will transfer nega-tive thinking and training in attempts to prepare women for the difficult possibilities that may arise on the job. I've had bosses tell me things like, "Don't trust anyone, especially women. There's no team. Take credit for everything your team does. Nobody is your friend; they're your subordinates. If they don't deliver, you burn them. Don't give 100% because you'll be taken advantage of." The list could go on and on. You may have been mentored or trained like this, but the buck can stop here. This is not how GSDers use their voices. We use our voices to encourage, empower, and ensure fairness and equality, not just on the job, but in all aspects of life. The late, prolific writer Maya Angelou once said, "I did then what I knew how to do. Now that I know better, I do better." We all have a responsibility to do better, and I'm hoping that you will take that responsibility seriously and choose to speak in ways that improve the lives of those in your sphere of influence.

I want to be clear about this concept of using our voice for good because I know there are times when we want to use our words in retaliation. I'm aware that people can be jerks. However, we don't have to match that bully's energy. It can stop with you. I know that is hard to accept for some, but there is good news. Nobody has to be a bully. What if we changed our outlook, knowing that our voices are our strongest weapons? How would that change our interactions in our personal lives, the interchanges professionally and around the world? We hear about pollution and toxic waste. If positivity has such an impact on our brains, how we operate, and how we live our lives, isn't using our voice as a negative influence going to be just as impactful on the next generation?

For the sake of the next generation, I want to address what we can do. We have talked previously about the use of our voice as the strongest weapon and the hyper-importance of speaking positivity into the world. We have always taught our kids that life has choices and consequences. We have taught them that everyone was born in the image of God, and, therefore, we are to show kindness, love, and respect to each individual in the world. Even when we don't agree.

What has really saddened me during the pandemic is people's seeming lack of respect for individuals' and families' choices. There is not a right way or a wrong way to live life. History has shown what has happened to empires where everyone lives, thinks, and acts the same. I don't know about you, but that's not the world in which I want to live.

This lack of respect and value of individuality prompted my family to equip and empower our kids with the verbal phrases and keywords they can activate when they are exposed to negative interactions. For us, it's not about eliminating the negative interactions, it's about having the tools and resources to be prepared for whatever bullying comes along the way and being able to cope and survive. My husband and I do the same thing that my dad did when preparing my sister and I for those fundraisers. We role play with our children. We go through possible conversations that they might have with their peers when they have disagreements. This is one of the ways we choose to set our children up for success. We know we can't shield them from all the negativity in the world, but we sure can give them a heads up on how to speak up for themselves and shut that negativity down.

As adults, we have to prepare ourselves for that same type of negativity. It is time for us to get out of our own way. It is time to be kind humans. Positive humans. To raise nice and respectful tiny humans. I would advocate that we must bring awareness to the negativity in the world and start moving the needle back to positivity. Our brains, our lives, and our futures depend on it.

Be a kind, adult human. If you are an adult bully, STOP! Evaluate your life, your words, your choices. Are you happy? I would imagine not. Think about what your new life would look like with a positive outlook, having a "There is always something to learn from every experience in life" outlook and echoing that perspective in the words you use. That's living the GSD Factor life, using your voice for good and not being a _____. We all have a choice in the words we speak, so let's take that sentiment to heart and speak words of life, power, and positivity.

But wait, let's not forget to do this for OURSELVES! It's not enough to just shut down the negative words from others, but we also have to confront and correct the negative things we say to and about ourselves. Positive self-talk impacts your thoughts and, therefore, your mindset. Furthermore, it is safe to assume that in order to create GSD Factor habits, we need to have positive, GSD Factor self-talk. Antonio Javar Hairston, in his book, *The Center,* talks about the importance of positive self-talk: "You are with yourself all day. You are thinking thoughts all day. It's vital that you create positive self-talk with yourself! It doesn't matter what's happening in your life. This will benefit you in any situation." In order to embrace the idea of being confident, we must reconfigure our thoughts to support this ideology. I can't stress enough that the GSD Factor is a mindset, so allow that mindset to change how you use your voice. Once you begin using your voice to speak positively to yourself, you'll have no problem using your voice to help and encourage others.

GSD moment of reflection

Answer these prompts in the space below or on the GSD Factor Hub:

Is your voice a force for good? Is it serving others?

_____

_____

_____

What's an example of positive self-talk that you practice?

_____

_____

_____

Is your voice used to harm? What if you were to change that? Could there be a different outcome?

_____

_____

_____

www.gsdfactor.com

A SPACE TO DREAM BIG . . .

A SPACE TO DREAM BIG . . .

PASSION AND DEDICATION

Everything up until this point has been about who you are and how you show up in the world. We've discussed the importance of being confident; embracing your true, authentic self; and using your voice to empower yourself and others. All of these qualities play an important part in living the GSD Factor life. Let's be real. It's hard to get shit done if you're not confident in yourself and your ability to use your voice effectively. Additionally, being confident, living your true, authentic self and using your voice also work interdependently with our next topic of discussion – passion and dedication. Having these first three attributes in place prepares you for finding your passion and building the dedication it will take to pursue the things that align with it.

What's the difference between passion and dedication?

Passion is the GSD Factor attribute that equates to the fire in your belly to get shit done. It's the love of something so deep that you can't imagine not doing it. If asked to sacrifice something for your passion, there is zero hesitation. It comes to you as natural as breathing. You go to sleep thinking about it. You dream about it, and in the morning, you have fresh ideas about it. Your passion does not feel like work to you. No matter how tough life is, you show up. You dig deep for it. You are striving to improve it. To be the best you can be.

Oprah Winfrey says, "Passion is energy. Feel the power that comes from focusing on what excites you."

I'm passionate about many things – obviously about being a mom and raising well-rounded tiny humans into well-rounded adults. I'm also passionate about advocating for the underdog, helping others find and live their passions, honoring my authentic self and my family's legacy, and finding ways to better myself. These are the things that motivate me, that make me want to jump out of bed in the morning and get going. What about you? What excites you? What is the thing in your life that still gives your energy despite spending hours and hours working on it? Through that passion and energy, there is great power that unfolds in your life, in the universe, in your companies, and in your community.

Dedication is the GSD Factor attribute that serves as the grit and the stamina driving your passion to the point of excellence and greatness. It's the drive in your life that says one job or one passion is not enough. It's the drive that says working an eight-hour day is settling. It's the attitude that consistently goes above and beyond, arrives early and stays late, even on weekends. It's also the wisdom to know when to rest and recharge.

Many years ago, my co-workers and I had just completed building a brand-new CRM. CRM, or "customer relationship management" is the system that companies use to manage and analyze customers' data and interactions. Upon completing our CRM and merging multiple instances into one, the data migration went sideways. It was a perfect storm of everything going wrong: the backups were corrupted, and the data got truncated. The platform/ product support team had never seen anything like it. We were facing an uphill battle. My developers and analysts were trying to avoid what we all knew was going to be the inevitable – a complete rehaul. In today's day and age there are now amazing tools that do the validation and can revert the data back to the minute, but in the mid 2000s that wasn't the case. We were going to have to go in and manually fix and validate each and every record. We mobilized an incredible team of dedicated individuals that were passionate about clean data, an accurate system and the success of the project. This team showed their dedication by not backing down from the enormity of the project before us. We developed a plan for cleaning the data; we stuck to that plan, despite the long hours and meticulous work, and we got it done.

That, my GSDers, is passion and dedication in action. We even had other teams raise their hands and step up to volunteer to help. They knew the importance and the gravity of the situation. They knew we could not fail. They knew that for our organization to be successful, we all had to roll up our sleeves and get into the trenches to get shit done. And that, we did. Fifteen people basically worked for three straight days/nights over a holiday weekend because this was the CRM for a multiple billion-dollar organization, and when they returned to work Tuesday, it had to be up and running. It was hard. It was grueling, but we got it done.

I think passion and dedication is the thing that you rely on even if you aren't sure of your direction or path. It's the thing that you fall back on in those moments when your future is uncertain, especially when you are walking down a path that others intended to use to hurt you, push you out, or ruin your reputation.

One of the most poignant memories I have of a time in which my passion and dedication to my profession were challenged is what I'll call the New Year's Day project. As I mentioned in the introduction, completing the project itself was a feat, but there was a lot more behind the scenes that made it even more challenging. I had just returned from one of my maternity leaves. I had worked for this company before, left briefly, and came back as head of business solutions. After almost three years of making improvements to streamline some of the processes, including the implementation of DocuSign that I mentioned earlier, the company was now treating me with extreme hostility and blatant disrespect. I am convinced, to this day, that it was all as a result of my pregnancy. Everything had been going fine until I announced that I was pregnant. One of the major projects I had been working on for the company was set to be completed right before I would take my maternity leave, and though I had put plans in place to ensure the success of the project even with my pregnancy, my team seemed hell-bent on sabotaging its timely completion. As fate would have it, I went into premature labor, and the team decided to go live with the project after I gave birth. My return from maternity leave was not met with positivity and warmth. Instead, I had been stripped of my role, responsibilities, and projects and had even been moved from the executive floor to another floor and into an office that had been repurposed as the furniture closet. I was so mad. I was so hurt. I felt like I was being punished for having a baby, ironically, at the hands of other women and moms! I had dedicated so much to this organization. I led trailblazing initiatives that propelled them forward in the insurance, technology, and financial institution space, and here they were treating me like an outsider.

Those early weeks after I returned, it was my grit and determination that said this will not be the thing that takes me down. My dedication and tenacity were on overdrive. Each day was a battle to look for the joy in staying. Each day was a test, another story that I could share with other moms that had experienced what I had experienced. Each day was me walking out the GSD Factor for myself, my family, my colleagues and, especially, for those that did these hurtful things to me. I kept showing up each and every day, and it drove them crazy. Some said to me, "Why don't you leave? It's embarrassing. I'm embarrassed for you." Others said, "You should file a discrimination case." Even the hotline and my lawyers advised me to do so, but I waited and still showed up. I was patient.

I won't pretend that it was easy. It wasn't. I won't say it didn't affect me. It did. At times it caused me to question my decision to pursue my other passion of being "Mom." It was lots of therapy and processing the hurt. I tried to understand why they would treat me in this way after having given so much over so long. I had to really change my mindset to be able to still show up. My GSD Factor

Clan was there, though, speaking truth to me, encouraging me. Through that, I was able to see this experience for what it really was. I was able to see what my story could be and would be. I began crossing paths with other women that were walking through the same thing, and I had to lead by example. My story was inspiring them, giving them hope, empowering them. I had to keep going for them. I had to keep going for myself. I had to keep going for my daughter who may choose, one day, to be a mom in the workplace.

I wanted to prove that workplace bullies would not win. You might strip someone of their roles and responsibilities, remove them from the executive floor, uninvite them from every meeting so there is nothing on their calendar. You can take away any and everything from the GSDer in the organization, but the truth remains. My passion and dedication for operational and technology excellence and for getting shit done even when the headwinds were strong. Deciding to leave on my own terms and not because imposter syndrome runs through the executive team with whom I previously worked. These were all real driving forces behind my refusal to cower to bullies. More importantly, I knew that they still needed me. The fact that they knew that too made them crazy, and I was here for it.

Sure enough that day came. They needed me. The company needed to complete an internal audit for a major financial institution. We had to build over twenty-five policies and procedures related to data for this organization. The project called for us to create the policies and procedures for anything and everything related to information security, firewalls, networks, etc. It was a huge task with many moving pieces. There was an enormous amount of work to be done, and though my work environment was hostile at the time, those in leadership knew that this type of situation was where I thrived. I had proven myself over and over again to be a person who worked well under pressure. I was the fixer, the only one who could come into a chaotic situation and restore order. That was my modus operandi. I had been the fix-it girl for so long that "fix it, solution, problem solver" were in my job description. This situation would be no different. The project was handed to me around Thanksgiving, and we were given a deadline of January first. Dedication, in this instance, meant working an enormous amount of overtime hours, including weekends and holidays. I don't recommend this kind of work schedule at all times, but we all knew that we were up against a tight deadline. We made that sacrifice because we believed in each other, and we wanted to see this project through.

In the aftermath, the audit was a huge success. I had endured the coldness of a hostile working environment, but my passion and dedication would not let me deliver anything less than excellent. I was motivated by my passion for motherhood, my heart for the underdog story, and the legacy of my family's greatness. My GSD Factor confidence was in full effect, and no amount of office politics was going to make me perform at a level that wasn't my usual high-quality work. The auditor commented that our audit was the best one that he had ever seen in his thirty years of experience. As for the naysayers, the leaders that assigned me the impossible so that they could have an easy reason to let me go were speechless. When it came to my performance evaluation, I was still in the top percentage of the organization. My favorite comment from the skeptics was, "You were supposed to fail. How the hell did you pull this off? We gave it to you late on purpose. We gave it to you over the holidays, and we didn't approve your vacation. We gave it to you in hopes that you would let us down, in hopes that we could fire you. We hoped that we would fail the audit, make you the scapegoat and seek damages afterward." My response to this person was, "Even after all these years, you really, truly didn't know me. You know that I GSD. You know that I come from ancestors of GSDers. Did you really think this tiny little audit was going to take me down? How wrong you were. And how dare you, another woman, another mother do this to me? You are going to have to try harder than that to get rid of me!"

Nelson Mandela says, "There is no passion to be found playing small - in settling for a life that is less than the one you are capable of living."

Passion and dedication are a powerful force to be reckoned with, and once you know your passion and what you're dedicated to, you gain even more confidence. That increase in confidence makes it much easier to be comfortable with your uniqueness and authenticity as well as your ability to use your voice. Can you see how all of this works together? Passion and dedication are especially powerful when you are certain about them both. You can run one without the other, but when you run with both, it's nuclear. It's game changing. It's life changing. The energy behind it makes people speechless.

Passions change, and that is okay. If they didn't change, I would be worried. My passion started with dancing and all aspects of that. When that was no longer possible, it moved into business. That's where I became passionate about being a leader, mentor and a coach. It's still my passion today. It's that passion that drove me to write this book. It's that passion that prompted me to start multiple companies on the tail of a pandemic. It's that passion that moved me to share my story because my voice is my strongest weapon, and there may be someone who needs to hear it.

For those who are reading this and are walking a path similar to mine, you are not alone. You've got this. Rediscover the passion and fuel that gives you energy. Rediscover the thing that wakes you up in the middle of the night. Unleash that dedication, those above and beyond actions. Passion + Energy + Dedication = unstoppable action. Your confidence goes to another level when you add in these additional attributes. Your trajectory is unstoppable. You are driving at a level that makes people tired just watching you.

I'll run with you. What pace are we setting in your GSD Factor life?

GSD moment of reflection

Answer these prompts in the space below or on the GSD Factor Hub:

What is your passion?

_____

_____

_____

Does your passion need a reigniting?

_____

_____

_____

Is your passion current, or is it time to change to better align with your values?

_____

_____

_____

www.gsdfactor.com

A SPACE TO DREAM BIG . . .

A SPACE TO DREAM BIG . . .

ACTION PLAN

HOW TO BE CONFIDENT

Be confident. The sentence is simple, but the concept is rather complex. This first, and possibly most important GSD Factor attribute is composed of three smaller tenets: Knowing and embracing your true authentic self, using your voice, and finding your passion and dedication. Once you identify and embrace all three of these tenets, you can lead by example with assertiveness, giving you a sense of empowerment and boldness. Moreover, your passion and dedication will motivate you to get shit done in all areas of your life. You may not have all of these tenets working to their optimum efficiency in your life right now, so let's look at one way that you cultivate and nurture these concepts in the meantime.

With my coaching clients that want to improve their confidence and assertiveness, I tend to recommend role play, coaching, or even acting classes. When faced with a difficult situation or conversation, role-playing can be an effective way to prepare for every scenario. My mom and dad did it with me all throughout my life, and it has worked. You can do this alone or with your co-workers, friends, or family members. Whatever the circumstance, role-playing allows you to practice the tone, volume, and authority of your voice.

Here are three steps for role-playing:

1. Think about the situation or conversation and write out all of the possible scenarios that could develop, including the opposing side of things. This will give you an opportunity to have a response ready for a variety of comments. You can't predict the future, but this will bolster your confidence as you prepare for the conversation. You won't feel like you're going into the situation blind.

2. Get with a partner or teammate and talk through every scenario that you listed. It is helpful to work with a teammate because you will have real-time feedback on the quality and effectiveness of your arguments and comments.

3. In addition to practicing with a partner or teammates, it is also helpful to practice in the mirror. This will make you aware of your body language and facial expressions. If you're confident in how you look, you'll be more confident in what you are saying. You would be surprised how helpful this can be.

My business partner and I practice this skill all the time as we prepare for meetings, especially proposals and negotiations. We list as many of the questions that we would ask if we were on the other side of the negotiation, do research to answer those questions, and practice the ways in which we will respond with each other. We even prepare in this way on written communications, so we know how to respond quickly should there be a counter.

For those of you that aren't sure who you are or want to uncover your true authentic self, there are amazing resources and tools at your disposal. Find your preference, and start with one resource, one book, one podcast, one webinar. Once you take that first step, the universe will bring you the resources and people you are supposed to meet. Once we truly know who we are and are embodying personal awareness, our ability to be confident starts to come to life.

Visit www.gsdfactor.com to join our GSD Factor Hub where you can take the Be Confident assessment that will provide prescriptive recommendations based on where you want to ignite confidence in your life.

ATTRIBUTE TWO

BE **INQUISITIVE**

The capacity to always be learning, ever the students of life. To walk in humility knowing that you are not the smartest person in the room but know how to mobilize the right team and people ensures that you are open to the fullness of life.

"

The greatest thing about tomorrow is, I will be better than I am today...There is no such thing as a setback. The lessons I learn today I will apply tomorrow, and I will be better.

—TIGER WOODS

"

ALWAYS LEARN SOMETHING

There aren't many things that I know to be absolutes in this world. However, I do know at least one absolute fact: no one person knows everything. Even though there may not be one source to reference for all of life's questions, I'm a firm believer that you can learn something from every experience.

I think this is what my parents might have been trying to teach me and my sister, when, at an early age, they exposed us to so many mediums – speakers, seminars, books, and articles – and encouraged us to learn.

My sister and I often laugh about how we weren't the kind of family that listened to music on the way to swim meets or dance camps. Rather, we were the family that listened to whatever book on tape or motivational speaker Dad liked at that time. We spent countless hours of road time listening to motivational speakers, business books, and self-improvement gurus. So much so that she and I loved to fly because it meant that we had our Walkman (for my young readers: that's a player that holds a cassette tape) with our music and not one of Dad's choices! Our parents introduced us to the likes of Zig Ziglar and Steven Covey, at the ages of six or seven. As an adult, I later found out that my dad shared those tapes with others in our family as well. (My cousin told me years later that he once got a speeding ticket because he was listening to Zig Ziglar tapes that my dad had given him. Apparently, he had gotten so motivated and was in the zone from the tapes that he completely missed that he was speeding. Dad would be proud.)

But we didn't just learn through hearing. Dad was always finding ways to expose us to different learning environments. I remember my parents taking my sister and me to the old success seminars of the early 1990s. My more seasoned readers may know the ones I'm talking about. It was at the old municipal auditorium in Nashville, Tennessee, and our homeschool assignments for the day were suspended because of a field trip. My sister and I were thinking we would go to the zoo or the museum, but nope, our parents took us to the success seminar. We were the *only* children there, and my mom, sister, and I were three of *few* women there. As a young girl sitting in a sea of men in suits, I got to hear Margaret Thatcher, first ever female, British prime minister. To this day, I can remember her poise, her articulation, her ability to captivate the audience and speak with authority. She embodied a GSD woman and inspired me in so many ways. Additional speakers I was honored to hear in person were Christopher Reed, Zig Ziglar, Colin Powell, and many others, and I often think back to those experiences.

It was through my parents, through the success seminars and exposure to authors and musicians I might not have otherwise listened to, that I learned the importance of omni-dimensional opportunities to engage with readers of all ages, and the great learning that can be gleaned by observing and absorbing others.

As a mom of two in the 21st century, teaching my children looks a little different in that I can expose them to podcasts, shows, and so many other things in a virtual experience. There are still books, of which my kids have many, and I love them all, but I also think it's great to learn by experiencing someone live, in real time. Never underestimate the power of talking to someone live on

Zoom, in person, or in any interactive experience. Having some-one speak into your life in a true, authentic way is powerful.

I'm not just a strong believer that you can learn something from any experience or medium, I'm walking evidence that it's true, whether it's your own experience or something you hear along the way that makes an impact.

So, how do we learn something from every experience? One thing I like to do is that after I have encountered or lived an expe-rience, I facilitate my own debrief or retrospect (for all my Agile Scrum masters out there), a postmortem of sorts. I ask ques-tions of others and of myself. Did I accomplish what I set out to do? What could I have done better or worse? How could I have responded differently? Did I listen? Was I heard? Did my point of view come across?

At one point in my career, I was looking to get out of my cur-rent position because I was looking for a new challenge and new opportunities. I had been at that company for a lengthy amount of time and had been looked over for a promotion, which would have made me the youngest director in the history of the organization. I was told that, as a girl, I needed to mature more. This "girl" was a married woman by that point with over a decade of experience, so you can imagine that comment didn't quite sit well with me.

I found the next opportunity and wasn't quite sure if it was exactly what I wanted, but I decided to take a leap of faith, more out of desperation, to get out of my current role. I got the job, and with it came immediate red flags: a role change, a boss change, and my responsibility doubling without compensation, but I pushed through. After a year, life transferred us to a new city, and my exit strategy was laid out before me. However, what I learned in that short amount of time became lasting life lessons, the first one being not letting desperation motivate me to move prematurely. Another lesson I learned was not to be afraid to negotiate. Ask for what you want, and don't automatically take the first offer. Those lessons have served me well and helped me to realize that every experience has learning potential.

Several years later, I was preparing for another transition. This time there was a similar sense of desperation in that I had just been laid off, and the whole country was facing a pandemic and looming recession. I found myself in a position of uncertainty, and once again, a learning experience presented itself. This time, it started with the interview process. For example, this interview was conducted via video conference because of the pandemic, and my interviewer, the company's CEO, was interviewing me while walking around a pool, dressed more for the beach than a job interview. Had I been interviewing for a summer camp counselor position, his attire would've made sense, but for Head of Technology, not so much. His line of questioning was all over the place, and he seemed to be promising the world. Additionally, it seemed strange that he would offer me a position that would require a fairly big leap in responsibility – Director of Business Solutions to Head of Technology. Granted, I was confident in myself, but the gap was glaring. Despite that and other red flags, I pushed on through. Afterall, I am Misha Bleymaier-Farrish, and quitting is not in my DNA. Remember, I'm the GSD woman, so if anything, I was either going to bring about change in the organization or learn how to adapt.

The time spent at this particular job wasn't always ideal, but the experience was invaluable. Though I didn't make the same mistake of not negotiating for my worth, I still took the position out of desperation instead of trusting my gut. The interview didn't feel right, but I accepted the role anyway. As a result, I experienced many obstacles and injustices that could have been avoided. There was a bright side, though. If it weren't for this position, I wouldn't have grown as a technologist and a product innovationist. I wouldn't have grown as a leader. I wouldn't have improved how to assess people or organizations during the interview process. I wouldn't have been able to add these lessons to my playbook and say, "I've been there, done that, got the t-shirt".

Not all learning opportunities have to appear as lessons either. Perhaps the lesson isn't a lesson at all, but a divine opportunity to meet someone in that situation or job who might later become a friend, a business partner, or spouse. I'm living proof that these things happen. While working for the company that subjected me to the harassment, bullying, and mom discrimination mentioned in previous sections, I met my husband. His first introduction to me was during a meeting in which a co-worker and I were facilitating a fix-it session. I was in my element and on form, so my husband got to see the raw, unedited version. Obviously, he wasn't too shaken, because after playing together alongside my father in a company golf tournament, we became friends. A couple of years later, we were married. My time at that company was fraught with many negative experiences, but had I not been there, I may have never met my person. So–worth it!

The GSD Factor mindset is one that suggests that we look at our experiences as glass half full, not half empty. Many people say that I'm so positive, and how do I always look at life like the glass is half-full? I think it's because my mindset is always on learning something from every experience. Even in those less-than-optimal situations, those negative situations, there is something to be gleaned. There is something to be stored in the playbook, to be able to recall and replay at a moment's notice.

In addition to recognizing that there is a learning opportunity in every situation, life has also allowed me to develop the ability to determine whether a lesson is one that will teach what TO DO or what NOT TO DO. I have had lots of mentors and heroes from whom I have learned both sides of this equation. I believe we can look to those in our lives, both personally, professionally, or from a distance and ask, "What can I learn from you, so that I don't have to live it?"

Many of these WHAT NOT TO DO lessons have come from people who served as leaders or supervisors for me in professional settings. One leader was specifically impactful in showing me what not to do, mainly, because she was a woman. On one hand, I admired her for her ability to have obtained and maintained a position of power in a male-dominated work environment. She was thorough and knew how to produce. However, some of her methods were questionable. Yes, she got shit done, but it was at the expense of her co-workers' respect and, ultimately, her humanity. During my time working with her, I learned not to make promises to people because there was always the possibility that they couldn't be kept. I also learned not to sacrifice my relationship with my family for professional success. I would see her stay longer hours than necessary at the office, and I saw the negative effects that choice had on her marriage and her family. Working with her was stressful, and as a woman, it was unsettling to have to experience this kind of leadership from another woman. All was not lost, though, because the memories from the time I spent under her tutelage still motivate me not to make the same mistakes.

Perhaps throughout your life you have had relationships that were chosen for you or that you encountered that weren't always the best. Maybe they came with a lot of toxic or negative interactions. Within each of these moments you are faced with two choices: you could be bitter or angry because you have to engage with those people, or you could choose to look at their lives or choices from a different view point.

For those people throughout my own life, as much as I want or pray for them to show me how to do things, sometimes, in their own brokenness, they could only show, demonstrate, or live their lives as examples of what not to do. They learned things the hard way, but that didn't mean that I had to learn those lessons too. I could learn from watching and observing them – the same way I could watch and learn in those success seminars. Sometimes these observations and interactions presented themselves as lessons on how to act or engage with others or how to handle diversity. These countless interactions, throughout my childhood and professional life, meant that I learned a lot through absorption and observation at early ages.

The dynamic between my late father and me was a great example of this type of interaction. My father and I didn't always have the best father-daughter relationship. It was messy. It was complicated. We certainly had some precious memories that I will treasure, but it wasn't an easy relationship. We both had to work hard. At times, we took breaks from it, and that's okay. We were both broken people, and that didn't always bring out the best in us. Towards the latter years of my dad's life, we were able to get really honest. In one of these moments of truth, I said to him, "I love you. I will honor you as my father because that's what our faith calls for. You will always be my dad, but there are times, in my life, when you have taught me more of what not to do than what to do."

These words, as honest as they were, were not the easiest to say, and they weren't the easiest for him to hear. However, in his last letter to me before he died, he acknowledged them. He was grateful for the reconciliation we had worked so hard for. He acknowledged that my words were true and that he was sorry he couldn't have done better. He asked that as I was able to continue to live my life and grow my family that I wouldn't forget him, that I would share stories with my kids about their Papa Teddy, and that I would be sure to share not only the good lessons, but also the lessons he wished he had learned earlier.

I chose my Orthodox faith for the fullness of the faith, a faith of the senses, a faith that says we need to lead a daily life of walking in and walking out forgiveness to ourselves and to others. That moment of acknowledging that someone in your life, be it a family member, coworker or boss, is actually teaching you what not to do can be extremely impactful. That's when you have to confront the tough, unblocked, unfiltered realities of life. The fullness of those lessons makes a much greater impact on our lives than we may realize. I think, in this society, we just expect that we are going to be taught what to do, how to do it, and get all the steps to success explicitly. It's less popular to look at a situation and ask, "What did I learn not to do?"

That's where this GSD Factor mindset of learning something from every experience originates. Are you living your life to the fullest? Are you living it out through all your senses? Are you walking a path of humility that says, "I know a lot of shit, but I also don't know a lot of shit." Do you walk into a room thinking and believing you are the smartest person there? Whether you are or not, I challenge your ego to take a seat. Listen to those around the room. What can you learn from them? How can you demonstrate GSD Factor leadership? GSD Factor leadership displays confident assertiveness while accepting the humility that you are not the smartest person in the room – that you can learn what to do and what not to do from the highest levels in your organization down to the entry-level positions. You can learn SOMETHING from everyone.

People often ask me when this lesson or lens of life started for me. The earliest time that I can remember is when I was diagnosed with late stages of Lyme's disease and given less than three months to live. Prior to my diagnosis, I had been on a pre-professional path for ballet and modern dancing, was part of a trailblazing, pre-professional dance company, and was in training and preparation to go dance for the Royal Ballet of Canada. Then everything came to a screeching halt. I had been experiencing unexplained physical challenges for about a year. I lost a good deal of weight, which started rumors of an eating disorder, and then I gained a good deal of weight, which resulted in being overlooked for dance opportunities. The strange part about the weight loss and gain was that I had not changed my diet or physical activity enough to warrant such changes. Additionally, my flexibility began to decrease. For a dancer who was known for being exceptional at leaps and turns, I began having trouble completing the simplest of jumps or turns. I kept going to the doctor, and though they weren't sure what was wrong, they advised against continuing in dance to avoid the possibility of doing permanent damage. My parents, who were concerned about the physical and emotional damage I was enduring, agreed, and just like that, my dream was gone. My expected future was gone. I was fighting to live. Fighting to breathe. Fighting to move. I couldn't possibly understand why I was going through this. I couldn't understand why God would allow something like this to happen. My aunt wrote something on a post-it note that will stay with me for the rest of my life. It said, "Maybe the lesson is how to BE, not Do. You are a DOER by nature. Rest in being a BE-ER. Maybe this season is about learning to Be and not Do."

My first response was, "Are you kidding? I'm a Bleymaier (and a Williams). We don't 'BE'. We are born "DOING". We helped a man walk on the moon. We built the first ever BLUE football field. We were the youngest organist to play in our parish church in Wales before heading to the Royal Academy of Music in the early 1900s. We built the first international music distribution network back in the eighties before technology made it seem possible, and the list goes on. We are DOers!"

Despite my family's history of doing, though, I had to pause. In that painful lesson of loss, grief, and trying to LIVE, I took one small step each day and tried to embrace this lesson of learning how to be. Now, I'm sure it was not the first lesson that I learned, but it was the most pivotal one I can remember. It was also not the first time that my life would suddenly and jarringly halt, putting me back at the feet of the lesson of *be* vs *do*. I embraced it, though. I held space for it and any other lessons that presented themselves.

At what points in your life have you been halted? Stopped? You were definitely going down one path only to have it completely cease. How did you evaluate, pivot, and relaunch? What did you learn from the moment? The GSD Factor mindset of learning something from anything makes these moments in life that much less daunting. It's never easy, but it's like muscle memory. Your body and mind say, "Oh, I've done this before. I've been here before. I know what to do. I know what not to do. I've got this."

Recently, I had the honor of being on the *Catalytic Icon Show* with host Melissa Unsell-Smith. I was on a panel with six other founders, and Melissa wanted us to share the struggles that we overcame as entrepreneurs. She wanted us to share our biggest mistakes as business owners and the takeaway or lesson that we would not want any other individual to have to live through. We even did a roundtable on what current pain points we were facing, and the rest of the panel provided insight to help. She had only found shows, podcasts, and seminars that talked about the positives and what to do, but she had not found anything *for* women *by* women that said, "Entrepreneur life is ugly, and we are here to share our story." It was a raw, authentic, real conversation with real solutioning. At that moment, I was even reminded that I wasn't alone.

As a GSD Mom, I have honest conversations with my kids. As a GSD boss, I have honest conversations with my teams. Also, being an Orthodox Christian, confession, apology, and forgiveness are woven into our faith and daily lives. So, after I act or speak in a less than ideal way, I'll turn to my kids or team and say, "I'm sorry for acting in this way; you have just witnessed how I should not have done something. Will you forgive me? Learn from what I just did, so you don't make the same mistake."

I believe if we demonstrate the kind of humility and awareness that we are living our daily lives being watched by our kids and our teams as they observe and absorb how to do things and how not to do things, our children will grow up with a balanced view of life. Our teams will witness a boss or a leader that is quick to apologize, learn, and do it better the next time. Parents are not perfect. People are not perfect. However, if we are honest and authentic with our kids and our teams, we have equipped them with far more than what to do, but also what not to do and the ability to evaluate both.

How many of you try and listen throughout your life because you never know what words of wisdom or lessons may unfold before you? We talked about the interactions with or observations of individuals in our lives, but I also believe that we can learn from a sign or a note (like I did all those years ago from my aunt's note), or maybe from a book, a podcast, or anything we see, hear, feel, touch, or smell. How enriched would our lives be if we took this approach of learning through our senses, all around us, learning what to do and what not to do?

I'm a big encourager of trying new things but in an A/B testing mode. That's my old marketing and technology coming out. A/B testing is known in the marketing and technology world as a comparison between two versions of a website or app to see which performs better. Users are randomly given access to either version, and statistical data is collected to see which version performed better based on predetermined criteria. I've found that this practice is good for more than just marketing and technology. Every time I encounter a challenge, whether good or bad, I recognize that I have the option to run my own iteration of an A/B test on the way I view the lessons learned from said challenge. In doing so, no experience, trial, or opportunity is wasted because I've analyzed the situation, considered various possibilities, and chosen the best path of learning and growing from it.

Guess what? This process can work for you too. Run an A/B test in your own life. Try, for a period of time, looking at life and every situation or interaction and asking yourself, "What did I learn to do, and what did I learn not to do?" I think you will be pleasantly surprised to see that it completely changes your outlook, and it completely changes how you react to those situations.

Life has continued to give me those interactions with colleagues or situations where the first thing I ask myself is, "What lesson can I learn here? Is it a lesson on what to do or what not to do?" This is one of the first lessons I coach on because if you can learn this, it completely transforms your outlook on life. My kids are young, but given that this is how I have always mothered, they always state to me, first, what was learned. What behavior should be adopted or not adopted? Like I said, I GSD in professional, personal, and even family life.

We have discussed at length the benefits of learning something from everything, learning what to do and what not to do, and the importance of having the humility to know you are not the smartest person in the room, looking at life as if the glass is half-full. The final thought I want to leave you with is the power of gratitude and coupling this with the other GSD Factor attributes. In *The Center*, Antonio Javar Hairston says, "If more people knew about the wonderful power of gratitude, they would complain less, and they would do it intentionally. Using your mind to look for gratitude is not only good, but it also brings good results for you and to you as well. The power of gratitude is that life begins to show you more things to be grateful for." The ability to see all situations, good or bad, as learning opportunities will help you to perfect the practice of gratitude. That's why being inquisitive and asking yourself what you can learn is such a powerful GSD Factor attribute. It takes intention, though. You have to train yourself to think this way, but doing so will allow you to see value in every experience.

My challenge to you is this. Look back on some of your inter-actions or engagements, recent or otherwise, and ask yourself, "What did I learn? Did I learn what to do or what not to do?" Ask yourself these questions from a place of gratitude, and it will com-pletely transform your outlook on the past and present. Learning from the past opens up opportunities for growing in your future. This newfound inquisitiveness will allow you a level of grace and forgiveness that will give you wings of freedom. You won't regret past decisions or mistakes because you will realize that you are still able to learn from those things, and these lessons will help you get shit done.

GSD moment of reflection

Answer these prompts in the space below or on the GSD Factor Hub:

What moment in your life taught you what not to do?
How did that shape you?

_____

_____

_____

What lesson from the past will stay with you for the rest of
your life?

_____

_____

_____

Is there something you are walking through right now that
you are struggling to see the glass half-full view?

_____

_____

_____

www.gsdfactor.com

A SPACE TO DREAM BIG . . .

A SPACE TO DREAM BIG . . .

YOUR CLAN

We are meant to have a community or a team. I like to think of this community as my GSD Factor Clan. I'm drawn to the word clan due to my Celtic lineage and ancestry across Wales, Ireland, and Scotland. In early Scottish history, clans had specialties or focuses like hunting, farming, sewing, or music. Within each of those clans, there were roles and responsibilities for each family. For example, a couple of families were the educators for the children, or the tradesman for the goods that were hunted, grown, or created. Whatever their role was within their specialty, every person had a purpose. They had a contribution to make, and this was well-communicated and known within the tribal clan and community at large.

You are the leader of your own GSD Factor Clan. No ifs, ands, or buts on this one. You, and only you alone, can fulfill this role and its responsibilities. As we embark on building your GSD Factor Clan, know that communicating to your individual Clan members that you consider them to be part of your Clan is key. Additionally, it's important, especially if it's a friend or family member, to ask them if they are willing to be part of your GSD Factor Clan. You are going to reach out to them. Look to them for guidance and feedback. Identifying, naming, communicating, and getting buy-in from your GSD Factor Clan will ensure your success as you are on this GSD Factor transformation.

Raised as a Liverpool FC fan, "You'll Never Walk Alone" was played and sung through our house and many family gatherings. The words ring so true: "Walk on, walk on. With hope in your heart. And you'll never walk alone." This journey called life was never meant for us to be alone or do it alone. When we are born, we are not alone. As we grow up, we experience different, sometimes difficult things that may make us *feel* alone, but it is important to believe and understand that, even then, we are never alone. Even in a world that has families separated by thousands of miles and the familial generational unit is less common, we still look to our families, those to whom we've been born and those that we have chosen. Iron sharpens iron. We can support one another. We know that we can learn from one another. We watch each other. We glean from each other's lives.

Your journey may have been less crowded than some, but at the end of the day, you had at least one person that helped you along the way. Fighter pilots don't just have a co-pilot, they have a wingman. That wingman is there to maintain formation no matter if it's in front, behind, or to the side. They are constantly watching out for the main fighter pilot and running interference if necessary.

Remember that your Clan members can come from everywhere and anywhere. Coming from a spiritual place, my faith teaches me that those that have gone before us are still with us, still praying for us and watching over us. So even in those moments when we feel that there isn't a single person in this world that we can look to, perhaps consider that there is a higher being and that we can look to our ancestors' lineage and legacy for inspiration. A favorite movie in our house is *Moana* for the music, the humor, and the story of Moana finding her true destiny, the destiny of her forefathers that had seemingly been lost. Her grandmother guides her to look up and look back to find her way forward. She encourages Moana that even when Moana feels like she is alone in her journey of finding her true destiny, she truly isn't alone.

There are a lot of different roles and responsibilities that each of these Clan members can take. From a GSD Factor perspective, I want to share with you the different types that you can consider:

- Your Spiritual member
- Your Mental Health member
- Your Self-Care member
- Your Physical member
- Your Hero member
- Your Dreamer member
- Your Execution member
- Your Cheerleader member

You may have several people that fulfill multiple roles, but each role brings a distinct value to your life. Your GSD Factor Clan grows and evolves with you as you are growing and evolving. We humans must continue to grow, learn, be stretched, and be challenged. Your GSD Factor Clan should do the same, and if it's not, then friend, it's time to evaluate and make sure they are serving you and meeting you where you are on your journey.

My biological family have always been the first members of my GSD Factor Clan. Before I even knew what this group was called, my immediate family was actively participating in their roles. My sister, for example, was probably my first execution member. She's always been like my right-hand. Not only could I bounce ideas off of her, but she easily anticipated my thoughts. This turned out to be advantageous because she could accomplish what was needed without me even having to tell her.

YOUR SPIRITUAL CLAN MEMBER

Family members are not the only people you can look toward to be a part of your Clan. As a matter of fact, you'll quickly find that people from all aspects of your life can fill these roles. My spiritual side recommends having a spiritual member. Perhaps it's a priest or pastor, or if you don't have a formal faith practice, then you can still seek out spiritual guides. I have two spiritual members. My first is my priest. He helps guide me through my Orthodox faith and serves as a source of wisdom and spiritual guidance for me and my family. My second spiritual member and I have a special friendship. Several years ago, I spent some time at a skete for a much-needed spiritual retreat. A skete is like a smaller version of an abbey or monastery. I developed this friendship with the abbess there, and she became my second spiritual Clan member. Ever since then, the abbess and I have been pen-pals. Though we've only been in each other's physical space once, we have maintained a friendship for over fifteen years. Her prayers and encouragement are always timely and effective. What a blessing it has been to have her in my life.

MENTAL HEALTH CLAN MEMBER

Be sure to think about soul, spirit, mind, and body and whether they are fully represented in your GSD Factor Clan. We have touched a little bit on soul and even spirit, but the mind is just as important. You need that mental health Clan member. It could be a therapist, counselor, personal coach, or even all of the above. I look to a couple of different people for my mental health, just as I do with my spiritual health. The first member is my therapist. The second person is a Tai Chi/Qigong master named Master Ou. He and I have been acquainted for several years, and he helps me by sharing meditations and movements from qigong with me. This practice is meant to support mental health through breathing, meditation, and movement. Over the years, Master Ou has coached me through these movements, and these meditations have helped me to recenter and keep balance between my mental and physical sides. I am grateful to have Master Ou and qigong as another part of my life.

As you are transforming on your GSD Factor journey, your mind must also transform. The GSD Factor is a mind-shift change and one that will bring about positive change. Sometimes, we can halt progress by overanalyzing. Don't get me wrong, thinking things through is a good practice to have, and we should embrace that. However, it is also important to employ balance and allow for creativity. Allow your brain to stretch beyond the confines of your analysis and challenge your own thoughts at the same time. Your mental health member will help you navigate this. Any transformation brings up the good, the bad, and the ugly. Being supported in your mental health is so important, and I can't stress this enough. We absolutely can do hard things, but making sure we have that support system as we do them will make it that much better.

YOUR SELF-CARE CLAN MEMBER

Similar to the mental health Clan member is the self-care Clan member who is equally as important. It's easy for us busy adults and parents to put our own self-care on the back burner and take care of everyone else around us. I know you've heard this before, but it's true; we can't take care of everyone else if we haven't taken care of ourselves. Think of what the flight attendants tell plane travelers as they're reciting the safety procedures. They always say, "Please put on your mask before helping others including your children." Then, they walk down the aisles, reminding every parent and guardian that this includes them. Why? Because as parents, our first instinct is to help our kids, but in a flight emergency, you must give yourself the oxygen mask first so that you can continue to help and serve your kids or others around you. We should think of self-care in the same way. It can address many areas – the soul, spirit, mind, and body, but be sure your self-care centers around loving, being present and extending grace and mercy to yourself – first. It may come as no surprise to you at this point, but I have a number of self-care members. My regular self-care members are my masseuse, esthetician, and hairstylist. Each one of these people is invested in my overall health, and they know me well-enough to be able to pinpoint possible causes for the changes they see in my muscles, skin, and hair, respectively. Our body lets us know when something is wrong, and my self-care members help me translate what my body is telling me. The time I spend with them is a time of relaxation and rejuvenation to keep me on my GSD Factor journey.

YOUR PHYSICAL CLAN MEMBER

Next, is your physical Clan member. This is a great time to share an example of Clan members who serve in more than one capacity. Master Ou, who I mentioned as a mental health Clan member, is also my physical Clan member because qigong incorporates both mental and physical practices. In addition to qigong, I've found that walking, barre, and Zumba are all physical activities that I enjoy and help me be the healthiest version of myself. Your physical member encourages you to get your body moving in some way. That could be through walking outside and embracing nature and the energy that comes from that. Are you a runner who turns off your mind and focus once your feet start hitting the pavement? Your physical Clan member could also be the physical trainer that is pushing and stretching you, making sure you are the healthiest version of *you*. This member could also be a yogi that wants to focus on your breath and the cleansing and centering that breathing brings. Some people even consider their Fitbit or children to fit this role because both those channels remind us or require us to stay active in some way. For my *Grey's Anatomy* fans, Meredith and Christina always looked to their "Dance it out" parties. What's your dance it out party? What's your physical go to? Whatever it is, it's a part of your life. There is scientific evidence that supports that physical exercise is beneficial to our bodies, minds, and emotions, so do not neglect this member!

YOUR HERO CLAN MEMBER

The hero GSD Factor Clan member is who you aspire to be. It could be someone you know or someone you don't know. It could be someone that is alive or has passed. I have two hero Clan members. They are both women who made profound impacts on my life as a woman navigating the business world. One is the recruiter who helped me land my first corporate job, and the other was someone I met by happenstance while traveling on business a number of years ago. They are my heroes because they inspired me to be the best version of myself. Your hero should do the same. Their story strikes a chord with you. You get excited when you talk about them. Perhaps they have achieved things in their life that you want to achieve. Perhaps their character, integrity, poise and how they handled situations is how you want to handle it. Again, it could be what they did, as well as how they did it. Find your hero. Study them. Learn from them. You have heard me say that I believe every experience in life teaches us what to do and what not to do. I believe the same is true for people. We can learn from their words and actions. We learn what to say and do and what not to say and do.

YOUR DREAMER CLAN MEMBERS

Now let's talk about the dreamer or the visionary GSD Factor Clan member. You've probably already figured out that I'm a self-prescribed big dreamer. Professionally, I can vision-cast with the best of them, but personally, I find it slightly more difficult to just dream, without immediately attaching practical limitations to said dreams. Enter my husband. At the beginning of our marriage, he would suggest dreams and goals for us as a couple that my rational mind would never imagine. However, his confidence and vision has inspired me over the years. Though it's still more challenging for me to dream big in my personal life than professionally, watching some of our visions come into fruition as a couple has empowered me to have the same freedom and confidence to dream big for myself.

The same may be true for you. If you struggle to dream or cast a vision for yourself, find that person that will be your dreamer and your visionary. At my consulting firm, we host these sessions called Dream Big sessions, and we help individuals and organizations take stock of where they are currently and where they want to be in the future. Many times, they don't know what that future looks like, so we facilitate exercises to unlock those dreams and visions. It's just like a muscle or a habit. We can get so caught in the daily rhythm of life that we forget to dream, forget to think about the horizon and possibilities. When we dream, it unlocks the hope of possibility. It unlocks creativity. It unlocks what could be.

YOUR EXECUTION CLAN MEMBERS

With any dream or vision, you need a plan to execute. This is where your execution GSD Factor Clan member comes in. Just think, you know where you are today and you know where you want to go, but do you have a roadmap or plan to get there? You need the map with the milestones that need to be hit in order to achieve. This person is your execution master, task manager or project planner. They will guide you, remind you of what needs to be done to reach that dream or vision in the timeline or date you set for yourself, and assist you in completing these goals and projects. I mentioned earlier that my sister played this role for most of my life and still does, as much as she can as an adult with a family and career of her own. I also lean on my best friend as an execution member. She's one of those people that I know I can call when I need an extra set of hands or just a sounding board for ideas or future plans. As with all of the GSD Factor Clan positions, this execution member will really be unique to your life and needs. Your execution member could be a personal assistant that helps you with scheduling or a baby-sitter that helps out with your tiny humans. Whoever it is, this person helps you get shit done in the most literal sense.

YOUR CHEERLEADER CLAN MEMBER

Many times, people associate their encourager or cheerleader with their execution master, but I would argue you don't, necessarily, want them to be the same person. Your cheerleader is the person who allows you to express your feelings, hears your cries and screams. Your cheerleader helps pick you back up, dusts you off, and reminds you of your dreams. They remind you to take it a task at a time; they remind you to commit to self-care and love you no matter what. They listen. They remind you to pause. They remind you to be present. Then they point you in the direction of the GSD Factor member that you need to work with on the next thing. If your cheerleader is also the person that holds you accountable and encourages you to move forward, then maybe they can be the same person. For example, one of my best friends serves both roles for me, which is completely natural, seeing that she is one of the people who is in the trenches with me. I also think that there is overlap from my spiritual members as well. Ideally, everybody in your Clan will be cheering you on and encouraging in some way, but it's good to know that you have a few people that you can go to and always get support and motivation.

This GSD Factor Clan is important, and I've given specific examples of who these people are and what they bring to my life to show how imperative it is to get the input of others. This second GSD Factor attribute is based on being inquisitive – being curious, asking questions, soliciting the knowledge and wisdom of others. Success does not come to people in isolation because no one can obtain success strictly off of their own skills or merit. Living the GSD Factor life means being fully aware that you do not know everything, nor are you the best at everything. We are all gifted with different talents and aptitudes. The healthy GSDer knows that and is not hesitant to tap their Clan members on the shoulder for help when necessary.

Now this brings up another great point and question that I often get asked. "Is your GSD Factor Clan paid or unpaid?" There are so many factors that go into this response. Are you doing this for your personal or professional life? It depends on the member that you are wanting to engage. It depends on your resource availability. It also depends on your relationship. You may be a member of one of your member's clans as well, so the relationship is symbiotic. Be honest with yourself and find the best member to meet your needs and resources where you are at that moment. When I was first starting out, I sought out members that were friends, family, and free resources. Then as resources became more available, I shifted some of my Clan to paid members. Thankfully, the beauty of this GSD Factor Clan and how it evolves is that it can ebb and flow as you need it.

We all come from different walks of life, different industries, backgrounds and cultures, so what may work for some may not work for all. You probably already have an unofficial clan, but if not, I want to encourage you to build, whatever that may look like, whatever you need it to be. This is a great time to pause, identify, and extend gratitude to your members, or maybe, it's time to change up your members.

Remember that some of your GSD Factor Clan members may serve in a couple of member roles, just as a few of mine do. For example, your self-care member might also be your physical member, or your dreamer is also your cheerleader. That's fine. This is your GSD Factor Clan. You get to build and pull together those clan members for you. And don't forget that what your GSD Factor Clan looks like today may not be the same needed for tomorrow. As you continue to grow in your GSD factor transformation, so will your GSD Factor Clan.

GSD moment of reflection

Answer these prompts in the space below or on the GSD Factor Hub:

What Clan member do you need the most and why?

_____

_____

_____

What Clan member do you need to roll off and why? What steps need to be taken to roll them off?

_____

_____

_____

Out of these: soul, spirit, mind, and body, which one do you need to give most attention to? What are two actions you can take towards that?

_____

_____

_____

www.gsdfactor.com

A SPACE TO DREAM BIG . . .

YOUR INSIDERS BOARD

Most entities in the corporate world, be they businesses, universities, non-profit organizations etc. have a board of directors. A board of directors is the governing body of a company. The purpose of these boards is to oversee activities, provide guidance and be advocates for the organization they are representing. Members can be elected, selected, or hired, but obtaining and maintaining a seat on a board is usually a sign that one's opinion and expertise is valuable and respected. Within the sports world, there is a term for a person in media that has connections, making them privy to information unavailable to others, literally the insider scoop of what is going on in that club or team.

We talked about our GSD Factor Clan and how important it is to have those people close to us and in place, but I also want to float this idea past you: If you were to assemble your own "GSD Factor Insiders Board?" What type of people would you pick? What kinds of things would you run past them?

Your GSD Factor Insiders Board is composed of a different group of people than your GSD Factor Clan. Your Insiders Board is made up of individuals that won't let you get away with your bullshit. They are the people that challenge you professionally, first, then personally, which is the opposite of your clan. Your

GSD Factor Clan makes sure that you, as a person, are developing, being nurtured, and holding space for the right things, be
they spiritual, physical, mental, etc. Your GSD Factor Insiders
Board will challenge your business decisions and strategies,
hold you accountable, and do anything to ensure your success
professionally.

I've always had a GSD Factor Clan, though its members have
rotated over the years based on my personality and growth. Take a
look at your Clan, and ask yourself, "Have these members rotated?
Are the members holding me back? Have they grown with me? Are
there too many new faces?" My Clan is a mix of old and new; some
have rotated off and rotated back on. It includes those that keep
me grounded spiritually, emotionally, and mentally. It includes
people that knew me when I was single and now know me as a
married mom of two. They come from all walks of life and have
proven themselves time and time again. In other words, they have
shown up.

My GSD Factor Insiders Board has also developed over the
years too, but it has definitely been more prominent since the
launching of my different organizations, Etymology Consulting
and GSD Factor. Originally, it was made up of people that I would
seek out for career advice, references, job opportunities, or it was
people who would refer and advocate for me. There were three
people, in particular, that served as my Insiders Board during the
early stages of my career. Two of them were my dad's best friends,
and the other one was the recruiter that I have mentioned in previous sections of this book. My dad's friends gave me business advice
in the areas of sales and marketing and have been great sources of
wisdom and guidance for me, especially in the years following my
dad's passing. They have filled that fatherly role for me and helped
me navigate some of the most challenging and pivotal professional
moments I've encountered. My recruiter, from the beginning of
my professional career, has given me invaluable knowledge about

interviewing, skills aligning, resume writing and has generally provided me with professional tips and tricks that have served me well as both an employee and employer. All three of them were my unofficial Insiders Board before I even realized what it was or how I could apply it to my professional life.

Once I had my first organization, Etymology Consulting, a global firm focused on a belief in actionable solutions with industry-leading innovation and a drive to give back to our communities, I realized the importance of having an Insiders Board as I was running a business. After starting this business, I began making concerted efforts to utilize the resources at my disposal. I needed help making decisions that would be profitable if I was going to be successful. I would reach out to my Insiders Board for strategic advice, go-to market experience, and industry practices.

My Insiders Board is a group of individuals that challenge me, sometimes daily, to think differently, not to settle, to remain focused on the right things at the right time. In the previous section, I mentioned how challenging it is for me to dream big in my personal life. I do not have that same problem professionally. I dream big, all the time. As ideationists and dreamers, we sometimes forget about what needs to be done in the present moment. If given the choice of creating a new product line versus closing out the financial books, we would much rather do the former. This tendency is a perfect example of why an Insiders Board can be helpful. Similar to my GSD Factor Clan, I have listed the positions that make up my Insiders Board. Some of them serve the same purpose as the Clan positions, but the focus is professional rather than personal. The roles are:

- Administrator member
- Tech and Data member
- Visionary member
- Execution member

YOUR ADMINISTRATOR BOARD MEMBER

The first Insiders Board member we'll explore is your administrator. The administrator is detail oriented, dotting the *i*'s and crossing those *t*'s to make sure things are as they should be. You could have multiple members of this type with specialty focuses such as legal, financial, etc. In some cases, your administrator board member and execution board member are one in the same, but this person is just making sure that whatever you are doing is being done with organization, flawless execution, and professionalism, all while remaining financially and legally friendly. Sometimes this member may be you. I fill that role within my organization as well as another member of my team who I rely on for help making financial and strategic decisions for Etymology Consulting as well as GSD Factor.

YOUR TECH & DATA BOARD MEMBER

The next member category is the tech and data board member. They will help you stay up to date on the latest technology platforms to keep engagement up or help you to understand what science and data is being researched and published. I have a few of these members. They are all people that I have worked with at other companies whose work ethic and expertise impressed me so much that I asked them to join me as advisors for my business. They accepted and are integral parts of my team. Depending on you and your Insiders Board, you may decide you need a separate technology and separate data board member, and that is ok. Out of all the members, this one could easily be a vendor that you engage with to handle all this. Whatever it is, technology and data are significantly changing each and every day. Your profession, industry, and company will help you determine the level of tech and data GSD Factor Insiders Board members you need.

YOUR VISIONARY & EXECUTION BOARD MEMBERS

These last two members – visionary and execution member – serve in the same capacity as the Clan members of the same name. The visionary member will help you dream big in your professional life and push you to make those dreams a reality. As I mentioned in the previous chapter, dreaming big professionally comes easy for me, so I am the primary visionary for my Insiders Board, but I get ad hoc advice from some of my other members when needed. Because I have so many big dreams and visions for my companies, I have a few different execution members, depending on the organizations' needs. These members keep me on track and help me actually carry out the plans and visions. I have an execution member for this book and other written content, marketing, and general business. As with the rest of your Insiders Board, your execution members are customizable and dependent upon your needs and your industry. Members will change as you grow and change professionally, so make sure you are constantly aware of what you need and how your execution members can help.

One of the great benefits of having a GSD Factor Insiders Board is having a group of people that can keep you on track and in pursuit of your professional goals. This book is a great example of a goal that has come about because of my Insiders Board. Writing a book was never on my radar, but by happenstance, a global media company found me on LinkedIn and expressed interest in helping me write a book. That interaction led to a meeting with the company, and after talking with them, I started to realize that I did have an interesting story that could help and inspire other people. Unfortunately, that company and I could not come to a mutual agreement concerning creative direction and other business specifics, so I decided not to partner with them for the book. I explored other options with hybrid and traditional publishers, but I soon realized that I wanted to do things differently. After months of research and seeking counsel from countless professionals in the publishing space, I decided to embark on self-publishing, not under my personal name, but rather, under GSD Factor Publishing. Soon, after informing my team, we embarked on this journey, but in true Misha fashion, I started sharing my journey with others. Consequently, within one week of this announcement, I had five other authors that were ready to publish under GSD Factor Publishing. I was starting to get caught up in the swirl of administration, setup, marketing, and securing these other authors when my GSD Factor Insiders Board intervened.

They firmly reminded me that I needed to finish my book first. That was the first and foremost step. We internally aligned on a plan to ensure that I got the time to write. They partnered with my husband and our family assistant to make sure that, for a short period of time, other responsibilities were handled, so I could write. I had to get my initial words down; my editor and book coach would take it from there. Once my words were down, I could embark on the operations perspective.

Having these types of people in your life that say the tough things at the right time is invaluable. There's nothing like a good dose of accountability to help you get shit done. I should know. Afterall, you are reading this book because my GSD Factor Insiders Board stepped up, showed up and spoke up, and I listened.

GSD moment of reflection

Answer these prompts in the space below or on the GSD Factor Hub:

What does your Clan and Insiders Board look like? What are the differences in your needs for them?

_____

_____

_____

During what event in your life would you have benefitted from having an Insiders Board that you could lean into?

_____

_____

_____

Maybe you already have a version of a Clan or Insiders Board operating in your life. Consider whether you have outgrown them or whether you need to make some changes.

_____

_____

_____

www.gsdfactor.com

A SPACE TO DREAM BIG . . .

HOLD WITH OPEN HANDS

Life is funny. One day, everything is going great. You feel like you're on top of the world, and the next day, or next moment, something can happen to change all of that. Suddenly, you find yourself in a season of darkness and despair. I know both of these seasons so well, and experiencing those great highs and crushing lows taught me the important lesson of holding onto things with open hands. What do I mean by that? Holding onto things with open hands means understanding and accepting that nothing is promised to any of us. While it is normal and human to find comfort in stability and consistency, it is also important to be flexible and open to the times when things are uncertain or aren't going according to your plans.

I first learned this lesson in my personal life through my experience with dance. I told you about my debilitating encounter with Lyme's disease as a teenager, and that's where this concept of holding on with open hands began. My entire life's trajectory completely changed within three years because of this disease. I went from being on my way to a thriving professional dance career to having to relearn how to walk! Each step in the recovery process taught me more and more about gratitude and not taking things for granted. With each new jump, turn and move I made, I embraced exactly where I was because I knew how easily all of that could be taken away. I was young, and the lesson was hard, but losing my ability to dance showed me how to be grateful and content with whatever I have or don't have and how to be open and available to whatever opportunities life presents. That's how I'm able to hold on to things with open hands today.

Concerning this GSD Factor life, I must warn you that if we hold on too tightly to things or people, we may be limiting our growth potential. One popular saying that I hear often is, "If one door closes, a window will open." It takes faith to remember that in the moment. When those doors close, it is time to channel the GSD Factor attribute that reminds us to ask ourselves what we can learn from these situations and how they can shape and mold us. That's when we need to decide if the glass is half full or not.

I can recall one particular example of having to hold things with open hands in my professional life. Remember the company that gave me so many red flags during the interview process? They offered me a position as Head of Technology, and I accepted it as a challenge and an opportunity for professional growth. Well, those red flags soon transformed into full-blown billboards of toxicity and hostility. I was working on the leadership team with a few ladies that suffered from extreme imposter syndrome, which they directed at me. Imposter syndrome is a pattern of thinking that can lead to self-doubt, insecurity, and negative self-talk. There are feelings of fear of being seen as a failure or holding back from reaching attainable goals.

Those that suffer from imposter syndrome can turn it inward towards themselves, but they can also project it onto others. Their manifestation of it can be cruel, nasty, and character-assassinating. The latter is what I endured, and it resulted in my burn-out. My team's hard work in the technology department put the company in a position to be bought in a multi-million-dollar acquisition. However, once that happened, the company's finances and spending habits came under scrutiny. Somehow, the other women on the executive team chose to use me as a scapegoat for high technology costs. I was subjected to daily inquisitions and constant harassment, even though I had more than enough documentation proving that every dollar spent on technology had been negotiated, approved, and the contracts signed for by the CEO himself, as he was the only one with this authority in the organization. This experience affected me emotionally, physically, and mentally. The harsh reality of how stressful the situation had become set in when my daughter asked me when I would have a job that made me laugh again and that didn't make me cry, a job that allowed me to pick her up from school and take her to karate, a job that allowed me to play with her and not always be working. Whoa! Our kids can be discerning, can't they? They listen. They observe. As a parent, I could have gotten mad at her for being sassy, but in that moment, she was speaking truth to me. This was the truth that I needed to hear. I knew I had to make a change.

When presented an opportunity to stay for a lot of money or leave, I chose to leave. Both the founder and CEO couldn't believe it. Why would I want to walk away from so much potential income? Why would I say no to working with the new organization? I had been the head of technology and had taken on the rebuilding of the entire technology stack with an unprecedented timeline in an industry-trailblazing move. The work and accomplishments that my team and I did garnered recognition from a national player in the industry who, later, bought us out for our technology. They wanted me to stay on board and assist with the transition and merger and acquisition activities as they adopted the technologies into their larger organizations.

I chose to walk away, and as that door shut, I showed exactly what it looks like to hold something with open hands, knowing that the best was yet to come. At that moment, I was letting go to survive. I was walking away to preserve myself. I knew I had a journey of healing ahead of me coming back from that burn out. The faster I got out, the better. There may be times where it may be helpful to hold that rhythm of you being a bad ass and the fact that you are a human too. It's about knowing, even through the tears, freak-outs, and sleepless nights, that when you wake up, you are still holding your conviction and commitment that what you are doing is right. It's not about being in denial of fear. It's about accepting it all and moving through it.

What if I hadn't said no? What if I had stayed? Have you stayed? Are you in a situation where you need to say no?

As a founder and entrepreneur of multiple companies now, I always tell my team we hold things with open hands. We are not afraid to say no to a client, project, or partner that doesn't align or doesn't serve us. Being willing to say no in those moments also means being willing to say yes in others. My editor likes to say that rejection is for our protection. A fellow colleague goes even further by declaring that every rejection is an opportunity to help someone else and grow ourselves.

Hold your Clan, Insiders Board, companies, opportunities, and employees with open hands. Open hands means that the right things flow in, and the wrong things flow out. Letting go of the wrong, negative, or toxic elements, always leads to greater growth, opportunity, beauty, and ultimately, success that you never dreamed possible. Basically, embrace where you are, but don't be so set and firm in those situations that you get all bent out of shape when different opportunities, challenges or unexpected changes occur. Rather, when life does start to throw curve balls, take that time to remember the GSD Factor attributes and be inquisitive. Ask yourself, "Why might this be happening? What can I learn from this? How can I grow from this? Is my current opportunity still serving me, or is it time to move on?" Those questions will help you release the hold you had on your security or your plans, all while you build character and increase in wisdom from the new challenges set before you.

GSD moment of reflection

Answer these prompts in the space below or on the GSD Factor Hub:

In what situation in your life do you need to see the most change?

_____

_____

_____

Are you holding onto something with too tight of a grip?

_____

_____

_____

Share a moment of gratitude for a moment where you let go and something new happened.

_____

_____

_____

A SPACE TO DREAM BIG . . .

ACTION PLAN

HOW TO BE INQUISITIVE

The key to being inquisitive is understanding that we are always learning. Your goal is to always be curious and remember to always be a student of life. Being inquisitive gives you the humble awareness that you are not the smartest person in the room, but the knowledge to know how to mobilize the right team and people to ensure that you are open to the fullness of life. We do this by always looking at life with a glass half-full approach and by searching for lessons in what to do and what not to do.

As lifelong learners, it is imperative to be surrounded by the right people, personally and professionally. Accountability makes everyone better, and that's the primary motivation for seeking out a clan and/or an insiders board. Some important points to consider when developing your Clan and Insiders Board are:

1. Your Clan is for your personal life. Ask yourself, "Who are the people who challenge me? Who do I call in a crisis?" Those people are probably your GSD Factor Clan.

2. Your GSD Factor Insiders Board is for your professional life. Ask yourself, "Who do I go to for career advice? If I lost my livelihood tomorrow, who would I call?" Those people are probably your Insiders Board members.

3. Having a personal clan or a professional insiders board requires you to act in humility. It takes humility to admit that you need those pieces of input, advice, and wisdom. It takes even more humility to honor and trust those opinions enough to implement the advice given, even when it doesn't feel good doing so.

4. Remember to practice gratitude when implementing a Clan or Insiders Board. Two ways in which you can do so are by offering to reciprocate or by serving as a mentor to someone else. Nothing shows gratitude like giving to someone else.

When it comes to your Clan and Insiders Board, it is important to note that you may only need one, or you may need both. The choice is completely up to you, but accept that as you continue to grow in your GSD Factor life, you may grow out of certain people. That is a natural part of growth, and it just means that some changes may be necessary.

Finally, the foundations of inquisitiveness are humility and gratitude. Keeping open hands and open minds are important because you never know what opportunities may present themselves or what escape or exit strategies you may encounter. Be humble. Be open. Be grateful for all the lessons life may bring.

Visit www.gsdfactor.com to join our GSD Factor Hub where you can take the Be Inquisitive assessment that will provide prescriptive recommendations based on where you want to ignite inquisitiveness in your life.

ATTRIBUTE THREE

BE IMAGINATIVE

The determination to dream big, never be
satisfied with the status quo, to be the innovating
solutionist, to continue to break down barriers
and say, "I'm here; what can we improve?
What is impossible that we can make possible?"

"

Don't be afraid to fail big,
to dream big, but remember,
dreams without goals are
just dreams.

—Denzel Washington

"

DREAM BIG

Dream Big. My team hears it. My clients hear it. My kids hear it. Imagination and dreams go hand in hand. For the first sixteen years of my life, my dream was dancing, but after facing sickness and injury, I realized that dreams could change. The injuries I incurred necessitated the change, but the experience just shed light on dreams that were always there – dreams of entrepreneurship, mentoring, and organizational leadership. I had been operating in those dreams all my life, but because dance was my number one priority, those other dreams just moved to the back burner. Being imaginative is all about keeping that dream-big muscle active and recognizing all the possibilities of your back-burner dreams.

As someone who is highly organized, follows rules, and has everything planned out, my ability to dream had to evolve. I've never had a problem dreaming; the difficulty came in allowing myself to dream freely, to resist the urge to be practical and logistical and just let my imagination run wild. Sometimes, I have to force myself to dream, but thankfully, I have people, like my husband, my GSD Factor Clan visionary member, that remind me to do so. I'm now operating fully in entrepreneurship and mentorship, so my dreams look different. They still involve a great deal of imagination, but now my dreams are all about being open to the opportunities that become available to me and knowing how to be in the moment. For example, I accepted an opportunity to serve on the board for a local organization that focuses on finding foster parents for teens. I never even knew this would be a passion of mine, but because I now dream differently, when the opportunity became available, I took it! That's just one instance of how this new way of dreaming has allowed my imagination to stretch and become a valuable tool in both my professional and personal life.

Perhaps that's why I've gotten good at helping people dream big for themselves and their organizations. I was at a hockey game with my husband, hanging out at our regular bar spot in the arena, and this group of fellow hockey fans joined us. We immediately hit it off and started talking about careers, jobs, and companies. There was one gentleman who commented that he didn't make a lot of money, but that his life circumstances really needed him to. I kept asking questions. I asked him about his vision, his ideal job, his ideal role, his ideal company. I was forcing him to introspect. He and I kept talking throughout the evening as he was seeking clarity and diving deeper and deeper with each question.

Through the course of questions and conversations, he was starting to think about things differently. What started as questions was turning into discovery and ultimately landing us on his Dream Big for himself. He said he had never thought about his skill sets in the way we were talking about them then, never thought about applying them differently to get a different outcome. Those questions began to plant seeds – seeds of hope, seeds of dreams, seeds of what could be. Some months later, he reached out on LinkedIn and wanted to let me know that that night at the hockey game of me not passing judgment and just asking questions ignited something in him that he had forgotten about. He was able to transform himself and find a job that was in more alignment with what he wanted and is now making two to three times more than what he was previously making. Our conversation (more like me listening and asking questions) over a couple of beers and hockey completely changed his life's trajectory.

When I think about the evolution of my dreams, I can see now that what I saw as a hindrance to my dreams – the way I leaned toward practicality and logic – could actually be an asset, as long as there is balance between logic and imagination. A major part of being imaginative and dreaming big is to figure out how to transform those dreams into reality. The best way to do that is to just allow yourself to dream. Let your imagination roam freely, but then access your practical mind and the ways to make the impossible happen. I know I've mentioned *Apollo 13* before, but let's look at it again. It has so many great lessons that we can apply to the GSD Factor life.

At one point in the movie, there is a CO_2 filter problem on the lunar module. The command module took square filters, and the lunar module took round filters. The command team were faced with connecting a square peg to a round hole using nothing but the limited resources they had available. The first step that the solution engineers took was laying out all the parts and pieces that the astronauts had available to them. This allowed them to dream big, innovate and come up with a solution to the problem at hand with the exact specs.

I have had lots of these experiences throughout my career. One time I was working with an organization where they had done the same manual-paper process for their direct mail campaigns for over forty years. Talk about a need for a change in mindset! It was a lot of work to get them to dream big. This was the same company that missed out on the opportunity to implement DocuSign before it was commonplace in the business world. Here I was, again, trying to get them to think differently about technology and processes. I wanted them to see that there is always room for improvement, especially when advancements in technology and business are happening at every turn and quickly. Unfortunately, though, this company's same lack of vision and imagination needed to take the risk on DocuSign was also at work with their direct mailing process. The process they were using required them to walk the campaign operations floor and count the folders in each of the baskets to understand where each campaign was. Reporting was a manual nightmare. If a folder got lost, there was no backup. It was an employee-management headache.

The craziest thing about this whole situation, though, is that it took us years to convince this department that they needed a change. They continued to present problem after problem. My team and I would put our heads together and present solution after solution. Sometimes it was a technology hurdle. Sometimes it was a timeline hurdle. Other times it was a process hurdle. Most times it was a mentality hurdle. My favorite exercise with them was to journey flow or process outline the entire workflow. When you journey flow, you utilize swim lanes that represent the roles and therefore each step, by each role, by each department are clearly outlined in their direct mail procedure from the beginning to the end. My office was a rectangle shape, and it was sixteen by six feet. We mapped out the operations on my office wall. By the time we were all done, their journey process took up ten of the sixteen feet on my wall. We then embarked on a twelve-month project to transform this manual-paper process into a digital workflow tool that was fully integrated with the CRM tool and main database, allowing for first time visibility and transparency. The automations alone saved the organizations hundreds of thousands of dollars. The data, analytics, and reporting that was now a possibility was enlightening and was able to provide actionable intel to the leadership team.

Soon after that project, we started to tackle their digital transformation. We were leveraging such old technology that what they considered to be the new technology for the project was over a decade old to the industry. We were trying to make something functional in the 2020s that was never supposed to leave 2010. This was the epitome of square peg, round hole, but we got it done. Am I proud of it? I'm proud to have led the initiative for digital transformation. I'm proud that after not having a digital presence, we finally got them one. I'm proud of the workarounds that my team built to make it look and function as best as possible even given the technology limitations. What probably frustrates me the most about that project, however, is that with a little more time, a little more budget, and vision from senior management, we could have made it so much more. We could have used state of the art technology so that we weren't setting them up at the technology launch date with the need to update right away. Despite all the hurdles, we met them where they were, and the experience reminded me that sometimes we have to focus on progress and not perfection.

Sometimes we have to lower our expectations to meet that of the client or organization. We have to be ok with good enough. It would seem that a perspective like this would actually be counterintuitive to the idea of dreaming big, but sometimes it is more productive to accept the idea of good enough. Just as I have expressed that I sometimes need help dreaming big in my personal life, I am aware that other people need help dreaming big in different areas of their lives. As a result, we all have to exercise some degree of balance and awareness of when to push those within our circles to dream big and when to just let them be. I have learned this balance in professional settings just by sheer experience. The skill of knowing when to stretch those dream big muscles will come with how well you know the organization or person, the set of circumstances surrounding the project or vision and how much stretching and dreaming they have already done. It will be different for everyone or every entity, but in order to grow and strengthen your ability to dream big, you have to exercise those muscles of imagination. The more you do it, the better you will get.

Let's look at the commonalities of my professional examples and what they show about being imaginative and dreaming big.

Well, they both teach us that it's necessary to approach things differently sometimes. At times, your solutions can only be found outside of the box, so we cannot be afraid to let our minds go there. We had to ask lots of questions to get to the root cause. We had to force people, who had done the same thing day after day for over thirty years, to change. We made them dream big. As you can imagine, I was not the most popular person on that project, but that didn't stop me. I had the vision for these people, for their teams, for the organization. I could see what this improvement could do. Even when they struggled to dream big for themselves, I dreamed big for them. Some thanked me and were grateful for it; others couldn't see the need and saw it as a waste of time and an annoyance. Change is hard and I get that.

Those are both normal responses to people who dream big. However, another outcome of having a dream-big person in your presence is that, eventually, that characteristic will rub off on you, just as my husband's ability to dream big has rubbed off on me in my personal life. That's a major benefit of having those types of people in your space. What an exciting thought to consider! I believe that you can dream big for someone or an organization, so they have something to look towards while you are asking questions, triggering those thoughts and mind patterns as they are reconfiguring their own brains in the dream big world.

"Your vision must be so strong and so real to you that it moves you to the action that changes your life," says Antonio Javar Hairston in *The Center*. "A great tool to use is visualization. I've always believed that if you can see it in your mind, then that is the first step to creating it. Seeing it in your mind is a wonderful way to set up a powerful vision for what you want specifically."

As I facilitate these dream-big workshops around the world, I always ask the participants, "If you didn't have to worry about budget, timeline, resources, regulatory requirements when building this solution, what would it look like?" Sometimes you have to start at the future state, then work backwards. If something is being so dramatically changed, it's not going to work to start at current. Figure out the future state and then lay out the roadmap to get there. Knowing when you need to start in the future state or start in the current state is a big first step.

With dreaming big you may at times experience failing big. Sometimes we must fail in order to see how dream-bigs become reality. Yes, we use our imaginations and do our best to plan and execute those plans in hopes of the best possible outcome, but dreaming big necessitates the awareness that every plan will not be successful on the first attempt. This is part of the beauty of the whole process. When you dream big, you give yourself permission to make mistakes. That's what most people and companies are not willing to do. It's a risky process that takes tenacity, endurance, and stamina to be successful. It is a risk, and it's not easy.

Once again, we can look at an *Apollo 13* quote for reference. There is a particularly poignant scene where Gene, leader of the flight crew that brought the Apollo 13 back to Earth after its oxygen system failed, says, "Failure is not an option," in regards to the fact that they had to get the astronauts home no matter what. He seemed to be dedicated to the idea that they were going to try every possible solution to get those men home, and that's all there was to it.

I have always shared this quote as one of my favorites for a couple of reasons. In the process of completing a project, I actually want my teams to try and fail fast and try again, but the ultimate goal, the ultimate objective, that ultimate date, that is what can't fail. I encourage my teams to see the process of executing the dream as a series of attempts at success. The project or vision didn't happen the way we envisioned on the first attempt. Okay, so we accept that, correct the errors and try again. That's how we reach success. This ideology was so impressed upon one of my vendors that they actually gave me the email address of "FINAO@(insertcompanyname) .com." Yes! I had my own "failure is not an option" email!

Why do I want my teams to fail fast and try again? It's simple. We learn quickly. It makes us agile. It teaches us to adapt and pivot. It causes us to realize what works and what doesn't work quickly.

One of the biggest moments of my career is when my team and I were delivering a working system for the national enrollment period. The organization had started from scratch with all their technologies, and we had to deliver a new operating technology by a certain date. Not doing so would mean we would miss the national enrollment period for insurance in the US. Failure was, indeed, not an option. Soon after I gave my "Failure is not an option" speech, I had some vendors rise to the occasion, and others bowed out saying they couldn't promise delivery. I respected them for it. Over the course of six months, we tried; we failed quickly sometimes, and we tried again. The important thing to remember, though, is that we kept going. We kept showing up because failure was not an option. I had industry experts tell us we were crazy. I had internal colleagues doubt us. Shit, we even had some parties try and sabotage us so close to the end because they couldn't believe we were actually going to pull it off.

I want my friends, colleagues, clients, and organizations to be bold, be brave and to dream big. I want them to take on challenges despite their insecurities, despite imposter syndrome, despite their education or lack thereof. I want them to dream big for their families and for their countries. I don't want them to be ruled by fear and stopped in their tracks. I once had a dear friend who had multiple businesses, one corporate with a side hustle that quickly turned into a stable revenue stream. She hadn't dreamed of what could be without a corporate job. She hadn't asked questions of herself and her team around the possibilities of building the side hustle. She, like many people, was paralyzed by fear of relying on her own company. She ended up working both her corporate and side business for over twenty years until, finally, one day she realized her side business was now her main business, and she could do it. Don't be that twenty-year person!

Be quick to identify those dream-big opportunities and seek out the help for your vision and the outline of the plan with the goals to get there. You'll know those opportunities when they present themselves because they will be the things that require sacrifice, discipline, and risk, but they are not impossible. These are the things that other people don't readily do because they're too different, too new, or too complex. Once you start pondering it, allow your imagination free reign. Go for it. Don't regret not doing it sooner. Even though the journey may have a lot of starts and stops, successes and failures, you'll learn quickly. You pivot, and you relaunch until you are at that success destination.

I'm on that journey with you. For example, being an entrepreneur and having the power to set my own hours has inspired me to experiment with different schedules for myself and my employees. Consequently, I'm working on a dream-big opportunity right now that involves me moving my company to a four-day work week. I know that's going to require some longer days for me and a more strategic and disciplined schedule, but I believe it's worth it. I'm making the necessary adjustments right now to make that vision a reality. That's how a GSDer makes the most of dreaming big. We use our imagination to see the dream in all its potential, make the plan, and then make it happen.

GSD moment of reflection

Answer these prompts in the space below or on the GSD Factor Hub:

What are some voids or needs you have discovered that spark your imagination for dream-big opportunities?

_____

_____

Think of a recent problem or challenge you have encountered. Did you use your imagination to solve this problem? If so, how? If not, consider how you could have used your imagination to address or solve this challenge.

_____

_____

Are there areas in your life in which you need help dreaming big? Explain.

_____

_____

_____

www.gsdfactor.com

A SPACE TO DREAM BIG . . .

A SPACE TO DREAM BIG . . .

NEVER BE SATISFIED

Because of my grandfather's history with NASA and the Space Program, I've always been fascinated and inspired by the Space Race of the sixties. As the country prepared for the challenge, President John F. Kennedy addressed the nation before the space efforts began back in September 1962. He famously said, "We choose to go to the Moon in this decade and do the other things, not because they are easy, but because they are hard." President Kennedy's words are at the crux of the GSD Factor attribute of being imaginative, and they coincide with the next sub attribute – never be satisfied.

We've talked about being imaginative as it relates to dreaming big, and never being satisfied is the next step to maximizing your imagination's potential. The United States' dedication to winning the Space Race is a great example of this type of ideology because of all the seemingly insurmountable odds that our space program was facing at the time. Many said it couldn't be done. Our space program was behind, very behind. The budget wasn't there. The infrastructure wasn't there. We didn't have the right leaders. We didn't have the right technology. As a nation, we needed technology for this program that had not yet been invented, and we couldn't even tell you who was going to invent it.

This wasn't a small project. It wasn't a digital transformation. It wasn't a new technology stack. It was putting a man on the moon and returning him back to Earth safely, which was a feat *no one* had done, and especially not with a program that was behind the technological curve. For example, in order to complete interstellar orbits, one of the first things we needed was satellites, and the first working satellite, Sputnik, was not created by the U.S., but by the Soviet Union. We basically started the race from behind. To add insult to injury, President John F. Kennedy addressed the nation with this challenge, "But if I were to say, my fellow citizens, that we shall send to the moon… and do all this, and do it right, and do it first before this decade is out – then we must be bold."

Talk about pressure! Think of how daunting a task that already was, but adding a timeline of fewer than eight years made it especially impossible. Still, with the backing of our president, our country and our citizens said yes. We embodied boldness. We innovated. We DREAMED BIG. There were many set-backs – losses to the Soviet Union on putting the first man into space and having him successfully orbit the earth and even the tragic and fatal explosion of the Apollo 1 in 1967, but the tide eventually turned in our favor with the Americans being the first to send a crew into space to orbit the moon. We didn't stop there, though. We weren't satisfied with just orbiting the moon. We had to land there, which we finally did in July of 1969 with less than six months left in the decade, memorialized by Neil Armstrong's famous quote, "That's one small step for a man, one giant leap for mankind."

As you can tell, I really fan-girl out on this story. If you're wondering why the space program is near and dear to my heart, it's because there are lots of connections between the moon landing and my career in the technology industry and GSD Factor. You could say it runs in my blood. The GSD Factor didn't start with me; it flows through my DNA, and it came from my grandfather.

I've mentioned him before, but it was his contribution and involvement to the space program that makes it a little more special to me. He was a part of the people who weren't satisfied with being second best. My grandfather said yes to the president. He said yes to his country by helping to train the astronauts who would eventually work on some of these special projects during this pivotal time in our country's technological history. He *dreamed big*. He has an award in the Smithsonian and his many decorations include the Legion of Merit and the Air Medal with oak leaf cluster.

In 2017, he was added to the General Schriever Wall of Honor at the Space & Missile Systems Center at Los Angeles Air Force Base, California. This memorial was constructed as a way to honor and recognize some of the earliest pioneers in space who have made tremendous contributions to our community, nation, and mankind. Each year a new class of names is added to the Schriever Wall of Honor. My sister and I had the honor of being there for the revealing of our grandfather's name on that wall. I was even more honored to have my own daughter, his great-granddaughter there as well. His immediate family was invited which included four sons and a daughter but given my dad's passing, the invite was extended to my sister and me. Sitting there surrounded by fellow Bleymaiers, hearing the accomplishments and achievements of Papa Joe Bleymaier I felt a great sense of pride, gratitude, and a weight of responsibility as if he was passing the torch of innovation on to my sister and me. It was the torch of dreaming big, the reminder to never say never, challenging the status quo and asking "Why not?" It was the torch of choosing possible instead of impossible. He passed this ideology on to his five children and sixteen grandchildren who will continue to pass it on for generations to come.

The drive of never being satisfied and never settling embodied my grandfather's life and mission and he passed this to me as one of the *key* attributes of the GSD Factor Life. I've also faced times in my professional career that had challenges similar to those that my grandfather had to face during the space race. One of those times came fairly recently, March 2020 right as the United States implemented the first mandatory shutdown on the country. We were facing, probably one of the most uncertain health crises of my lifetime, and because I had just been hired as the new head of technology for an insurance company with an emphasis in Medicare, my team and I were now being asked to make some pretty drastic technological changes as a result of this disease. The short version of our task was that we needed to rebuild, rethink, and re-engineer what technology would look like to serve the open enrollment community in the midst of a pandemic. Oh, yeah, and we had to do it in six months!

For the next several months, my team and I worked hundred-hour work weeks to build technology that would allow us to complete insurance quotes for clients and go through the enrollment process electronically. The technology was so innovative and game-changing that we started garnering the attention of our competitors, government agencies, and eventually buyers. The technology stack that we created was the catalyst to that company being bought in December of that year. That whole experience, though exhausting, further solidified the never-be-satisfied genes I inherited from my grandfather.

I know that I come from ancestors on both sides of my family that embraced and amplified innovation, drive, dreaming big, and never being satisfied, but I believe that this lives within each of us. Whether your ancestral history has examples of this for you to follow or not, you are responsible for your history, *your story*, the story that your lineage will speak about.

Ask yourself, "What should I never be satisfied about?" Whatever it is, try saying, yes, because in the words of famed American author and activist, Glennon Doyle, "We can do hard things." So don't avoid those difficulties or challenges. Tackle them head on with your imagination and that spirit of never being satisfied. Who knows? You may surprise yourself and impact history just like my grandfather and the ingenious men and women he worked with during the Space Race.

GSD moment of reflection

Answer these prompts in the space below or on the GSD Factor Hub:

What challenges in your life have you been avoiding?

_____

_____

How can you apply the concept of never being satisfied to those challenges?

_____

_____

What one dream do you have that you haven't allowed your-self to explore?

_____

_____

What dream-big goal do you want to try in the next twelve months?

_____

_____

www.gsdfactor.com

A SPACE TO DREAM BIG . . .

17

PROBLEMS LEAD TO SOLUTIONS

Everyone has problems, challenges that disrupt the overall enjoyment or successful flow of our lives. People have problems getting along with co-workers, problems saving money, problems maintaining healthy lifestyles. The list goes on. Everyone also *sees* problems. These are problems that are noticeable to everyone but can't necessarily be changed on an individual level. For example, we see problems with the environment, problems with the education system, problems in politics, even problems we see with our friends, family members, or co-workers. Problems are unavoidable. Whether at home, at work, among family, or among friends, we all face them. I believe, though, that the way we approach problems separates us into two types of people: problem-pointers and problem-solvers.

There is a great book by Kirk A. Weisler called, *The Dog Poop Initiative*, which provides a great lesson into problem-pointers and problem-solvers. The book's target audience is children, and its purpose is to teach young readers how to be proactive citizens who make efforts to better every environment they are in, even when they don't necessarily have to.

Essentially, in *The Dog Poop Initiative*, a dog takes a shit out on a soccer pitch. We won't address the fact that the owner didn't pick it up in the first place, but dog owners, you know who you are; do better. Over the course of a day, there are multiple soccer matches where parents, coaches, referees, and even kids are problem-pointers and even great problem-communicators to anyone that was coming to the pitch. The book goes on about how the pointers consistently and vehemently pointed at the poop. The communicators made sure to warn other people to avoid the poop. Some even complained about the poop. They changed where they played. They changed how they played, but no one tried to solve the problem. The author goes on to say that about 220 people avoided the poop that day, and, in the end, only two actually took action to scoop the poop. That's not even one percent. Seriously?! That's art imitating life, though.

Think about how many times you hear someone complain about a problem, and compare that with how many times you actually see or hear about people who take the initiative to fix a problem that is staring right at them? The time and resources spent by the rest of the population pointing it out, complaining, and over-communicating is staggering. What if, as a population and a world, we just moved that needle just a little, even to a full one percent? How different would our world look? How different would companies run?

Being a problem-solver and not a problem-pointer is one of the main fundamentals of living the GSD Factor life. If you find yourself on the solving side of that categorization, then you're probably a person who, as we know I like to say, gets shit done. Don't get too excited, yet because being that type of person comes with its own set of risks. If you're a natural-born GSDer, then you don't have a problem finding and implementing solutions to problems. You know how to use your imagination to dream big, and when it comes to problem-solving, you understand how important it is to never be satisfied. However, the real discipline for people who are born with the gift of problem-solving and GSDing comes when it's time to determine what *kind* of solution to use. I'm talking about the MVP, here. No, that's not the *most valuable player*. It's the *minimum viable product*. It's a term used in the business world that basically means a product that's going to give you the maximum amount of learning about your customers with the least bit of effort. To translate that for the purpose of problem-solving, it's figuring out what solution you can come up with that works and creates time for you to rest and prepare for a permanent solution. If an emergency comes up at work one-hour before you are scheduled to leave, what solution will allow you to address the problem and still make it home in time for dinner? Finding and applying the interim solution rather than immediately beginning work on the long-term solution is a skill that will serve problem-solvers well because it allows you the time to rest and avoid the stress of always diving head-first into long-term solutions.

Now, all hope is not lost if you find yourself on the opposite side of the problem-solver/problem-pointer coin. If you're not one of those people who immediately sees solutions, or perhaps you are a problem-pointer, it's okay. We are all works in progress, and you, too, can develop those skills and eventually become a master solutionist.

My high school instructor never gave out tests; he gave "opportunities." What if we thought about problems in the same way? If you think about it, you probably have "opportunities" every day. I have them all the time. One example of such an opportunity happened with one of our clients. The billing vehicle for one of our client's customers stopped working. You can imagine the level of freak out that was happening when they realized they couldn't bill their customers. Instead of freaking out along with them, I immediately realized that we could use this as an opportunity to upgrade the billing technology. I suggested that instead of just fixing the problem, we should provide an alternate way for them to bill temporarily, shut down the system, and use that time and money to upgrade the entire system. Thankfully, they agreed. Catastrophe avoided. When faced with a new problem, there's always the chance to ask yourself whether there's an opportunity presenting itself? Is there an opportunity for growth? Is there an opportunity for the company? Because we all face problems in every aspect of our lives, we can apply this forthcoming suggestion to any area, but for the sake of this platform, let's specifically address how we need to approach problems or opportunities in professional settings.

First of all, I like to advise people that if you're going to present a problem at work, then be prepared to also present a solution. Am I saying that you cannot express frustrations or difficulties with systems or processes? No, you most certainly have a right to your frustrations, and it's healthy for you to express them. However, there is a time and a place for everything, so I do suggest that if you need to vent about something, do it in the appropriate setting, to the appropriate people and in the appropriate manner. Otherwise, you run the risk of being perceived as the resident naysayer.

If you're good at identifying problems, how do you then turn towards becoming a problem solver? To be an effective problem solver, our mindset and state of being need to be unified and focused on peace. Anxiety is often our first response to problems or conflicts. Oftentimes, anxiety coupled with fear can block our brains from solutioning and finding the answers; this amplifies the fear, causing us to be insecure. We don't want to give power or add fuel to the problem, we want to work the problem. In my experience, I've learned that solutions and answers arise organically from an aligned peaceful state of mind.

For example, have you ever been in a situation that was stressful, and you couldn't think straight? I've experienced this kind of stress a few times, but it was particularly recognizable as we got closer to the deadlines of a number of major career-advancing projects. I was experiencing solution fatigue, which is exactly what it sounds like. My brain was tired of solving problems, so it would become increasingly more difficult for me to do so. When those times came, I didn't try to push through the fatigue. I would stop working and go for a walk or spend time with my children. Sometimes the most practical solution would be to go take a quick power nap. I love power naps! Those power naps work wonders for my weary brain, and when I wake up, I'm refreshed and ready to get shit done.

Why is this? For the same reason you need to shut down or restart your computer, your brain needs to reboot; it needs a rest. When you wake up, you are more likely to be in a peaceful state, and suddenly, ideas start flowing. My recommendation is having something by your bed on which you can capture ideas because as you are sleeping, the brain is recharging. You may wake up with a brilliant idea that you need to record before getting back to sleep. Finding a state of rest and peace is about groundedness. It's about finding a center.

Each person finds their center in their own way, but you have to come up with a wellness plan and strategy for yourself to be able to get back to your center. If finding that peaceful state of mind is a struggle, I recommend some meditations and visualizations to aid you in that process. I've often heard that peace is a state of rest and calmness in the soul.

Once you've found a peaceful mindset, presenting a problem with a solution can become much easier and more systematic. Before you can actually present a solution to a problem, it would be helpful to first identify the size and scope of the problem. To do this effectively, we need more information. We get more information by, first and foremost, listening.

One of the great attributes of a leader is their ability and willingness to listen. Sometimes we problem-solvers are so ready to jump into action that we don't listen and miss important pieces of information. If you can't tell, I'm a problem-solver, and there are many times when I have to remind myself to stop and listen. I exercise this skill on a daily basis with my team and clients. On a personal level, my husband and I have a phrase that we use when we are sharing problems that are going on. We say, "I need you to listen," or "I need you to help me solution." This came after a few times of us sharing with one another in hopes that the other would just listen, but instead, we jumped to solutioning. This usually caused us to miss the entire point and even propose the wrong solution because we didn't take the time to listen to the problem in its entirety.

Once you have a basic understanding of the problem, the second step is to focus on not being afraid to ask some clarifying questions. Depending on the temperature of the situation, you can ask, "May I ask some clarifying questions? It will help me navigate as I prepare a solution." If the moment is not right, revert back to listening, and come back to that person at a later time to gain the clarity you need.

Now that we have our problem, and we are gaining clarity through questions, we can continue to size and scope, which will help make our solution more effective. My daughter gave me a great example of this one day with some homework from her life skills class. Her school counselor used weather as the analogy for assessing problems and how to approach them. The scale she used is brilliant, and I've adapted the same ideologies to the business world.

- Windy = tiny problem, no biggie – Handle on your own.
- Rainy = small problem – Engage with a single colleague to solve.
- Stormy = medium problem – Engage with multiple stakeholders to solve.
- Tornado = big problem – Enlist executive help or sponsorship to solve.

Of course, work problems can be complicated and multi-faceted. I realize that the process of actually solving the problem may be a little more involved than this system of assessment, but you have to start somewhere. That first step of assessment can make or break how you address the problem. If you are successful in gauging the size of your obstacle, I believe you will be more likely to be successful in solving it.

Looking back at the billing system problem that my team and I faced, I realize that we followed these exact steps to resolve those technical issues. The client came to us in a panic about the situation; I combined steps one and two by making sure I stayed calm and relaxed while listening to their description of the malfunctions. Next, I asked several questions of them to figure out just how challenging the situation was, and my team and I concluded that this would require some executive help to resolve, making it a tornado level problem by my daughter's life-skills class scale. After making that analysis and getting approval from the necessary parties, we were able to correct the technical difficulties, which resulted in an upgrade in the client's billing system. I share these steps because they have proven effective for me time and time again. They come second nature now, so I just rinse and repeat each time a new problem arises. My hope is that you, too, will add them to your GSD Factor tool belt and reap the benefits when developing solutions for your own life.

I think we can all agree that problems and challenges are an inevitable, unavoidable part of life. It would be great if more people took the initiative to be problem-solvers, rather than just problem-pointers, but that's not reality. Actually, being a problem-pointer, in itself, isn't bad. There's value in being able to identify problems. However, if you're ever going to get shit done, you've got to be able to do more than point out the problems. Furthermore, becoming the person who can effectively assess and solve problems requires you to be imaginative and open to a myriad of possibilities for solutions. This is an invaluable skill and one that you will find to be helpful on your GSD Factor journey. This concept is like the culmination of dreaming big and never being satisfied. If you do those things, then you will find that solutions come much more freely than if not. That skill, effective problem-solving, will open many doors for you, both personally and professionally.

GSD moment of reflection

Answer these prompts in the space below or on the GSD Factor Hub:

Are you a problem-pointer or a problem-solver?

_____

_____

_____

Do you have a natural tendency towards one approach on the scale vs the other?

_____

_____

_____

What stage of the problem-solving steps do you struggle with?

_____

_____

_____

www.gsdfactor.com

A SPACE TO DREAM BIG . . .

ACTION PLAN

FOR HOW TO BE IMAGINATIVE

What does it look like to be imaginative in everyday life? It's a combination of all three sub-attributes: dreaming big, never being satisfied with the status quo, and using your imagination to develop and implement solutions. People who think like this are constantly looking for ways to improve. They yell out, "I'm here! "What can we improve? What seems impossible that we can make possible?"

There is no problem that doesn't have a solution. Even when we don't know of a perfect solution, the goal is to work the problem. It may not be the right solution immediately, but imaginative thinking can transform you into an innovative solutionist that isn't afraid to try and fail quickly. Innovative solutionists are persistent because they understand that failure is not an option.

Though the solutions may be born of imagination and creativity, the thought process for finding the solution can easily be broken down into a few actionable steps:

1. Center yourself so you can open up to those big dreams and solutions. What centers you? There are several practices that can be helpful for centering. Some people journal, exercise, create art, garden, etc. Whatever is necessary to get you to a place of peace and stability, do that. Pop over into the GSD Factor Hub where you will find some examples of meditations and visualizations that will, hopefully, jump start your peaceful mindset journey.

2. Ask questions. This is a part of never being satisfied. When it comes to dreams and ambitions, it pays to be inquisitive, curious, and constantly in search of knowledge. Ask yourself, how can I be better? What can we do to improve?

What are different ways of addressing or correcting this problem? Continue to push. Push for the next promotion, the next level of education, the next fundraising level. Your proclivity to improve will directly affect your level of success. You cannot get better if you are not constantly looking for ways to be better.

3. Initiate. Remember *The Dog Poop Initiative*. It is one thing to dream-big and ponder all the possibilities for solutions and improvements, but the real challenge is taking the initiative to put all of these thoughts and considerations into practice. Will you be a problem-pointer or problem-solver?

As you make these steps of centering yourself to dream big and asking questions and initiating, you will become more comfortable with being imaginative, and soon those big dreams will begin to turn into your reality.

Visit www.gsdfactor.com to join our GSD Factor Hub where you can take the Be Imaginative assessment that will provide prescriptive recommendations based on where you want to ignite imagination in your life.

ATTRIBUTE FOUR

BE **PRESENT**

The ability and willingness to keep showing up, even if for a moment; it's the art of starting to do something, anything and trusting that process even when it seems that there are more pivots than plans. It's also living with the attitude of progress, not perfection.

"

If you can't fly then run, if you can't run then walk, if you can't walk then crawl, but whatever you do you have to keep moving forward.

—Martin Luther King Jr.

"

KEEP SHOWING UP

In my life, there are a lot of areas where I have to focus on staying present and diligent, and many of these areas don't come naturally to me. What helps is that as an innovative solutionist, I've learned that I will never get it right the first time, but if I keep showing up, I'll find power in the journey. I realize I am not perfect, and there are certain things that I constantly work on improving in my life. One of those things is being a present friend. I tend to slip into coach or consultant or business mode easily. As a result, I don't have many personal friends, but I make a conscious effort to ensure that I am as present as possible with the friends I do have. Another area that I have to keep showing up for concerns rest. Though I am better at taking steps for self-care, like therapy, exercise, massages etc., I have difficulty doing nothing. That's right. I feel so much guilt just resting or chilling. I'm working on it, though. Lastly, if you would ask members of my GSD Factor Clan, some might tell you that I have trouble saying, "No." It's not that I'm a people-pleaser, but I think my tendency to agree to taking on projects or other tasks is directly related to my struggle to rest. These may not be the easiest things for me to improve, but I've made a conscious effort to work on each one, to keep showing up for myself, and to grow. Recently, I was asked to be an officer for one of the non-profit boards on which I serve. Though I was honored to be asked, I realized that I just did not have the time or energy to serve as effectively as needed in that position, and I respectfully declined. I shared that with a Clan member, and she was shocked. That decision allowed me to lean into all three of the areas that I'm working on improving. By declining to take on more responsibility, it means that I can stay present with the non-profit without being overwhelmed, that I prioritize my rest, and that I maintain space in my life to keep working on everything else that's keeping me busy and continuing to strive for work-life-family integration. That is progress, friends, and proof that if we keep showing up, we will see improvement.

Showing up isn't just for ourselves. My daughter's karate school requires that even if you are not actively practicing on the mats, you still stand ready and present, showing up for your fellow teammates and cheering them on, because sometimes just being there is enough. That's showing up too. Sometimes all you have in you is to cheer on someone else, and when you can do that, you're showing up for that friend. After blowing my knee out and destroying any possibility of me becoming a professional dancer, I made a decision to still show up for my students and co-workers at the dance school I helped co-found. Because of the severity of my injuries and the extra damage I did to my knee by continuing to dance on it for three more minutes after injuring it, I had to wait six weeks before the doctors would do surgery. Those six weeks could either be spent on bed rest or in a wheelchair taking it easy. I spent them in the wheelchair, but I did not take it easy. Instead, I showed up to class to finish out the year with my students. I taught as much as I could from the wheelchair, and when I couldn't teach or needed more help, my sister stepped in and demonstrated moves for me. It was a difficult six weeks, but that's what showing up for my students looked like. To this day, I cherish those days because they were the last days I spent as a teacher at that school. It was totally worth the challenge.

But what about when the odds are stacked against you? How do you keep showing up when it's feeling especially hard?

Have you ever heard the idea that bullies operate from a deep underlying root of fear? What does a bully hate more than anything else? Bullies hate when people show up and stand up for themselves and for others. I've been there too. I returned back to work after maternity leave to a working environment that was clearly meant to isolate and ostracize me. I was again faced with the option to show up or not. Even though I was removed from all of the projects I was on before I took leave, and even though I was removed from the executive team and prohibited from making any changes or decisions of impact, I still showed up to support my teammates when needed. I would give advice and support however I could. I would take time to coach and mentor others, and as a result, three coworkers that I mentored were able to use the guidance I shared to pivot into bigger and better positions. To be clear, I would have been justified in just going into my newly relocated closet of an office and pouting, but instead I showed up for my teammates. Those members of the executive team who were trying to assassinate my character and perpetuate the idea that I was a problem had a hard time making that narrative stick when I was still being a team player despite all of the obstacles they put in my path.

Showing up even in the face of adversity or just meanness is a lesson that I'm already teaching my kids. I let them know that they may not make the team or get picked for the play, but they should still show up to cheer on their team and fellow classmates, because showing up isn't just for ourselves. Just like my daughter's karate school practices the same theory, we can easily apply this on a daily basis throughout our lives and the lives of our kids and teams. This is what is remembered, and this mindset, when taught at a young age, can positively impact our industries for generations to come. It helps diminish some of the negative effects of the participation trophy mindset.

I struggle with the concept of participation awards in events where there is a clear winner and loser, because in life, we win, and we lose. We get the job, or we don't. Even when we lose, though, it's a character-building moment that teaches us that there will be losses in our lives, but that we must show up again. One such opportunity to show up in the face of adversity happened for me when a coworker and I were both up for the same promotion. The company ended up giving my coworker the promotion, and almost immediately, he called me asking for help on a project. I could have declined his request for help, but I recognized at that moment that he was still a co-worker and a valuable member of the team. It would be out of character for me to be petty and hurt the whole team because of a decision that the executive team made. That's not who I am, and that's not congruent with my values. Instead, I gave him the help that he needed, and he even made a position for me on his team. After the fact, the executives came to me and acknowledged that they made the wrong decision. That acknowledgement didn't change the promotion, but it was validation for me that choosing to show up for others, especially in the face of adversity, is still the best option.

Maintaining this type of ideology hasn't always been easy. In fact, there are not many easy days because there are negative stereotypes, perceptions, and opinions that challenge me on a daily basis. They haven't stopped me, though. My persistence has oftentimes made me the solo girl on the tech team or the solo woman in the boardroom, and yet, always I've kept showing up.

Let's shift gears for a moment and talk about the topic of imposter syndrome that has become a popular one in the corporate space. Imposter syndrome is defined as "a psychological pattern in which an individual doubts their skills, talents or accomplishments." There are two types of imposter syndrome sufferers that

I've encountered. The first is the person that suffers and struggles with that reflection internally. It causes them to freeze in fear and not take important steps forward. The second type of imposter syndrome that I've seen, firsthand, takes form in the person that suffers and struggles and projects that onto others, meaning they can't stand it when other people succeed because they don't want to be replaced, shown up, or measured against.

Being on the receiving end of imposter syndrome projection is psychologically draining, and before I left the company that was trying to push me out, I had to learn and adapt quickly to how I would interact with these types of colleagues. As you can imagine, my GSD Factor approach to work was highly annoying to them. Remember, bullies hate people who show up and stand up for themselves, and my continual support and help for my colleagues was showing that I would not cower to their antagonizing. Countless interactions with them were intended to be negative and hurtful because they were trying to make me quit. To the point where one got so fed up, they accidentally blurted out: "You keep f**cking showing up. You email. You are in meetings. You are on calls. You keep giving 150%. Why do you keep showing up? We want you to just go away." To this I smiled and said, "I don't know how not to show up."

But what happens when the imposter syndrome, and all the negative interactions, come from ourselves? I still deal with this type of imposter syndrome at times. It shows up most frequently when I have to pause, re-evaluate, pivot, and relaunch. In those moments, I feel like what I did the first time failed, so I really have to incorporate positive self-talk to combat it. The other time I really struggle with feeling like an imposter is when I'm interviewing for a job. For a long time, I couldn't even get an interview because of the lack of a college degree. I would always dread the college question. People didn't stop asking me about it until about year eighteen of my twenty-year career, so it had been a constant point of insecurity for a long time. Now, however, I quiet that voice of self-doubt by walking through my story and reminding myself of all the amazing things I have accomplished without a degree. Those things motivate me and remind me that I am enough and worthy of any position or opportunity that comes my way.

To those of you who are on that imposter syndrome journey, navigating it as a victim, I encourage you with this. Just keep showing up. Let things roll off your back. Like I tell my teams, "Duck it out." That means remain calm, cool, and collected while you are floating on top of the water. On the inside or under the water, however, your feet are paddling for dear life. I'm thankful that the worlds of mental health and corporate spaces are coming together to address something that has been a struggle for a long time. It's important to give this topic a space to discuss and work through.

As someone who has led teams and organizations through solutioning workshops, the key concept I consistently express is to keep showing up. You may not have an idea. You may not know the answer right away, but keep showing up. You may not have a contribution at that moment. Keep showing up to support your colleagues, your friends, your family and yourself. Even if you can't see the victory, you win by being there and not giving up.

GSD moment of reflection

Answer these prompts in the space below or on the GSD Factor Hub:

Where in your life do you consistently show up the most?

_____

_____

_____

Where do you want to show up?

_____

_____

_____

Where do you NEED to show up?

_____

_____

_____

www.gsdfactor.com

A SPACE TO DREAM BIG . . .

PROGRESS, NOT PERFECTION

Attention, GSDers and future GSDers! With all this talk about getting shit done, it would be negligent of me not to warn you about one possible side-effect of GSDing. As you start building the motivation to be confident, imaginative, inquisitive, and now present, you might start feeling pressure to reach perfection. First of all, what is perfection? I think of perfection as the expectation that mistakes are unallowable and unacceptable. The desire to want to perform to perfection or to create perfect outcomes is human and has its benefits, like seemingly flawless product and performance executions. It would seem that since I have already discussed the need to keep showing up, perfection would be the obvious reason why one would need to do so. That couldn't be farther from the truth. Be careful, GSDers, that you are not pressuring yourself to keep showing up in the pursuit of perfection. That's a slippery slope. Instead, I'd like to challenge you to embrace the concept of *progress not perfection.*

This is a much better goal post to target because it only requires you to be there. It's a given that anything you're doing will be excellent because you're already working on being confident, imaginative, and inquisitive. With attributes like that, the outcomes can't be anything less than amazing. Perfectionism can be subtle, though, so please make sure that you are exercising balance and realistic expectations when you show up. You do that by ensuring that you are constantly integrating rest and reevaluation in your routines. Know that being a work in progress is completely fine. Sometimes showing up means just that. You just have to BE. Sometimes *being* looks well-put together, organized, and efficient. Other times, *being* looks broken and in a complete state of surrender, but the important part is that you are there. You are allowed to give yourself grace for those times. Perfectionists don't extend themselves grace. They don't celebrate the wins because the target is always moving. They are never satisfied, but not in the way that precipitates more knowledge and growth; they are never satisfied in a way that doesn't allow for a break or a self-congratulatory high-five. Resting and being in the moment are foreign concepts. This can lead to burnout, and, GSDers, I've been there.

It was a crazy time in the world. Covid-19 was just starting to wreak havoc on the United States, and the whole country was in a frenzy. The government had just issued a nation-wide stay-at-home-order, and I had just been laid off because my current company wanted a break from innovation. They basically told me that I had been pushing them towards new things for four years and they needed a break. They didn't want to do any more investing in technology, research, new products, or new projects. I was the head of Business Solutions, so it was my job to push the company to try new technology, research, products and processes that would make the company more efficient and productive, so their desire for a break from innovation basically meant they no longer wanted me.

That declaration led me to my search for the next thing. What I found was a role that allowed me to dream big, and my boss and the leadership team were big dreamers too. This was it, a golden opportunity to be Head of Technology, a role and experience that I mentioned before, for a company who wasn't afraid to dream just as big as I wanted to dream. I have so many valuable lessons from that position, and this example is no exception. Whenever I would put a dream on the table, their reply was always, "Yes! What does that look like? Let's make it bigger. Don't worry about the budget." In fact, budget was never a conversation because in their minds, money was no object where execution of the perfect dream big idea was at stake. This was my ideal job: like-minded individuals that seemingly got me and my approach. For a person who was told there was no more desire for innovation, a company that trusted me enough to place me as Head of Technology was like a dream come true. I went from being in a position where I would normally have to wait around one year's time to get a new idea, technology, or process approved to getting approvals overnight. That's exactly what I was looking for – a chance to try things that had not been done, break new ground, do the unexpected. Sure, there was fear that it was too good to be true, but there I was, a female head of technology, under 40 years of age. That was a big deal. According to research, only 10.9% of leaders in the technology space are women in America. Similarly, only 21.4% of executives at large American insurance companies are women. I had beaten the odds. I was a mother of small children, under forty, and with no college degree, but somehow, I landed a position as Head of Technology for an insurance firm! I couldn't pass up the opportunity. Of course, that opportunity came with its challenges.

While I was excited to operate in this new position, what I hadn't realized or been exposed to before was a perfectionist big dreamer. It's important to identify the characteristics of a perfectionist big dreamer in order to avoid becoming one. A perfectionist big dreamer is someone that is willing to do the crazy, out of the box dreaming, but they either don't leave enough time for that idea to incubate, to take root, or be finished because they are already onto the next big dream. They also don't care for much prep time or scope time because they are afraid of analysis paralysis. They want to try, fail fast, pivot and try again. This seems like every big dreamer's ideal situation, but the perfectionist big dreamer never wants to try those dreams in small pilot situations. These types of people want to do things full scale because they strongly believe their idea is the perfect idea, and their hubris tells them that because it's perfect, it will work.

The CEO of my new company was a text-book example of such a person. Consequently, when my team and I delivered something, it was never good enough because the goal had shifted. I'm really proud of the work we did but having to complete it with a perfectionist big dreamer at our helm was a nightmare. The project was due in early October, and we worked tremendously hard for several months prior to that deadline to make sure we were ready. We delivered a full system to him ready to go early in September. The plan was to deliver at the beginning of September, train everyone for the month, and be ready by October. However, when we showed the project to our CEO he explained that it was no longer what he wanted.

That type of project delivery was standard procedure with our CEO. If the team rolled something out, we had to do it full scale and not in phases to test it out. Testing was not an option because that took too much time. Besides, why do we need to test the perfect dream-big idea?

This is probably the worst way to go about technology development. Releasing a new project takes time to test, train, ensure that everyone's access is working, and correct and a myriad of other things. We quickly realized that if our CEO would not allot this time for us, we would just build the testing phase into development without specifically calling it out. Fortunately, we had enough foresight to begin including a testing phase despite our leader's belief that it wasn't needed, but it would have been much more helpful if he would have just adjusted his perfectionist big-dreamer tendencies.

You can probably imagine that these conditions did not make for the best work environment. There was no such thing as work life balance or work-life-family integration that I strive so passionately for. There were long, twenty-hour-days with no breaks or downtime for the better part of a year. No vacations or holidays. It was go, go, go. Some were good pivots, and others were not great. There wasn't time to evaluate, research, or ensure requirements and compliance. Then my team burned out. The signs were glaring. The team wasn't willing to give above and beyond anymore; they pulled back and re-established boundaries. In hindsight, their re-establishment of boundaries was a lesson for me because I should've helped them set those boundaries in the first place. The burnout didn't just extend to them, though. I was also severely overworked and overextended because of this project. My desire for self-care decreased. I struggled to make time for anything, and I couldn't seem to step away from work. I was glued to my phone and email. Any time I missed a text or email, I panicked. I was at my breaking point. I had burned out.

There was a bright side to this burnout. Our hard work hadn't gone unnoticed. The company was being bought for one of the versions of the dream-big technology that we had built and demoed. Our CEO might not have been satisfied with the project as he had moved the goal post, but the buyers were. Now we were being sold, and the buying party wanted to know about the cost, testing, policies, procedures, the rollout campaign, and ultimately, the usage and adoption. They wanted the dream big but expected all the documentation that comes with the gift of time. Unfortunately, that was something that the perfectionist big dreamer didn't prioritize or think was important. That meant more work for us. Not only were we expected to deliver a finished project, but we also needed documentation to support the development as well. I then enlisted the help of another team to come alongside us and document simultaneously. During that time, I managed both teams;

we would do a release, and I would hand the release notes over to the documentation team. All the teams reported to me, which made for twenty-hour international clock days. I would say good night to the US team as our international team was waking up to start their day. Ultimately, we delivered what was needed but at the expense of my team's and my physical and mental health, and at the end of the day, it wasn't worth the emotional, mental, and physical draining it caused.

I included all of this because our burnout was a direct result of our leadership. So, if you identify with the plight of the perfectionist big dreamer, be careful not to overdo it. Watch yourselves; remain accountable and listen. Yes, you have big ideas, but at whose expense might these big dreams materialize – yours, your family, your organization or your team? Keep yourself in check, so you don't do more harm than good.

Meet my friend Lauren Martin, LPC-MHSP, podcast host of *9toKIND*, guest speaker on the GSD Factor Podcast, and thought leader on the topic of "Pep Talks for Burned Out Perfectionists and People Pleasers." I highly encourage you to go to her website and consume everything you can.

One of my favorite quotes she has is this: "Done over perfect my friends. If I embraced this motto in the past I would have started my podcast earlier, created content earlier, pitched my talks sooner, been in better physical shape, had more time with friends & family, traveled more, put that basket of laundry away. You get what I'm saying. Remember, perfection is subjective, and most of the time it's unattainable."

This is for you recovering perfectionist GSDers. Let this sink in for a moment. Perfection is subjective, and is, most of the time, unattainable because we are broken, fallen people in this world. Moreover, it would behoove people who struggle with perfectionism, to simply get good with good enough. Get good with leaving things for the next day. Get good with laying out your to do list or initiatives into three buckets of NOW, NEXT, and LATER. There will always be something.

We have begun tapping into the concept of good enough, but for now, let's focus on progress. *Webster's Dictionary* defines progress as "forward or onward movement toward a destination." Progress means you keep showing up. You are doing something, anything. You are moving forward even if it means a little. You just start even though you know it won't be the end result.

There are a couple of things you can do each day to make sure you keep moving forward. I've found that, as an entrepreneur, I need to make a few small, actionable steps each day like maintaining consistent communication with the necessary parties, be it via emails or text messages. I make sure things are filed away properly and that my social media and other online content is up-to-date. Again, the goal is progress, not perfection, and progress means trusting the process while you prepare for the opportunities that are coming. Continue to fill the pipeline even if the pipeline is washed out in a matter of a few days. Keep calling. Take a note from nine-year-old Misha, and keep walking up to those booths and book-sellers, little by little.

Now that we have discussed the importance of progress over perfection and the significance of making small, actionable steps each day, let's address the elephant in the room. What do we do when things are not going as planned? Maybe your plans and road-maps have not materialized. What now? Do we have to dream big for the next thing? Do we have to abandon and start from scratch? No. We go back to the basics. We go back to where we started, making little steps and progress each day. We lean all the way in. We are methodical. We set our intentions daily. We celebrate the little wins.

I've had several experiences that required me to go back to the basics. In one instance, I was activated by one of my partners who had a client that was in a 9-1-1 situation. The client had kicked off an integration project that included eight vendors, but none of the vendors had delivered a comprehensive project plan, timeline or to-do list. When I came in, the first thing I asked about was the project's current state, future state, and business requirements. I then asked every vendor for their project plans. After analyzing all the plans, I realized that the problem was not with the vendors, but it was with the client. The vendors provided reasonable projected dates, but the client wouldn't accept it. The vendors projected seven months, but the client wanted it in three months. She could not be reasoned with, and the vendors basically gave up on what the client wanted. The project had completely stalled in the middle of an implementation, and the lack of movement, being forward or backwards was critical to the global organization. Everything was chaotic. My immediate step was to answer some foundational, basic questions: "Who was responsible for what? What was the scope? What had been done so far, and what needed to be done? These basic questions and steps seem so simple, yet by walking this client through these questions and documenting everything, I was able to create a plan. As a result, we were able to begin executing and making progress. It was slow progress, but progress nonetheless.

I've had to complete this process for myself a few times. Whenever I no longer have a pipeline, projects, or clients, I go back to the basics. I spend time reaching out to people, networking, keeping order and process to my day. I make sure I'm organized and caught up on administrative tasks. I also take time to research and pursue other opportunities. Finally, I try to consistently network and apply for roles or projects. This practice has been particularly helpful for me as an entrepreneur. When things are not actively pursuing you, go back to the basics, working at them bit by bit, until you get your flow again.

Founder and entrepreneurial thought leader, Melissa Unsell-Smith of the *Catalytic Icon Show* talks about how the founder's mindset is so critical and important to entrepreneurial success. The founder's mindset is the set of foundational beliefs that serve under your company or organization. Many times, founders or entrepreneurs have to come back to this mindset when they need to reset and refocus:

The founder's mindset includes:

- Influence
- Zone of mastery
- Asking for help

Your influence reminds you of what impact you make to society. In moments of stress, ask yourself, "What is my reach and influence?" Then, think about your zone of mastery: what are the skill sets that you have and do well at? What have you mastered along the way? Often, when we are going back to the basics we can lean into our zone of mastery because it's well known, comfortable, and we are most confident doing those things. Then finally, consider the art of asking for help. Learn to know when there is either a gap in your time and execution, your goals, or your skill sets. Believe that asking for help is a sign of strength and surrender. Even if you have a firm grasp on the aforementioned ideologies, you can be sure that you will still run into difficulties as an entrepreneur or founder, specifically the temptation to be perfect. My experiences with a perfectionist big-dreamer CEO can serve as proof that perfectionism doesn't just affect the perfectionist. Its tentacles can touch all those in our sphere of influence.

We must constantly remind ourselves that we are works in progress, and remember, it's progression over perfection.

GSD moment of reflection

Answer these prompts in the space below or on the GSD Factor Hub:

For your journal prompt let's go back to what Lauren Ruth Martin said, "Done over perfect my friends. What if I had embraced this motto in the past I would have done...." What would you have done if you embraced "Done over perfect"?

_____

_____

_____

Is there a current project or problem in your life to which you can apply this "progress-over-perfection" ideology? Explain.

_____

_____

_____

What small, actionable steps can you make to keep your progress going?

_____

_____

A SPACE TO DREAM BIG . . .

A SPACE TO DREAM BIG . . .

BE PRESENT

Being a mom is one of the greatest opportunities I have been given. I am keenly aware of the fact that being a parent is a gift, and I feel so grateful and blessed to be able to walk this journey as a mother. I have learned to be sure that I'm present with my family, friends, and colleagues, but especially with my kids. I take all the GSD attributes seriously, but this one – *be present* – is especially significant to me because of the responsibility I have to my children to make sure that I am fully present with them as much as possible. My children have taught me and continue to teach me so much. Once you are open to the process of being present, you will be amazed at what you can relearn by looking at things through the eyes of a child!

Children are innocent because they haven't lived life. They don't have baggage. Their skin is thinner. I had a client once say to me, "I love working with young people because they are ignorant, and ignorance is creativity waiting to be tapped." How true that is. The next generation can bring a fresh perspective, a fresh outlook on things that we older generations have lost sight of.

My husband and I learn from our kids daily. It's not always easy, but we try to listen and learn from them as they are, hope-fully, learning from us. My clients hear kid stories all the time because they are so applicable to life and career. Gone are the days of children being seen and not heard. Listen to them. HEAR them. There is a difference. Slow down and be present with them. Look into their eyes and truly hear them. So often, we get busy with life, and we miss things.

One lesson I learned through being present with my kids centered around the idea that we should still be present and grateful for the beauty and goodness even in bad times. Since the death of my mother-in-law after her valiant battle with cancer, my husband has become the legal guardian to his mid-90s grandmother who suffers from late-stage dementia and lives in Memphis. This responsibility means that he will have to spend time in Memphis to check on her as well as managing her life and handling her affairs. On one particular occasion, she was rushed to hospital unconscious, and as a result, he had to rush to Memphis. She ended up being in the hospital for an extended period of time, which meant he would have to stay in Memphis overseeing her care. At the moment, we didn't know what this timeline would look like. We were taking it day by day. One weekend during this time, it was apparent the kids needed some dad time, so we piled into our car and drove the 200 miles to spend the afternoon with him. We were able to meet up at our friend's pool and clubhouse, and for a few hours, be present with one another and exit the reality in which we were living. We didn't know the date of our next reunion or if Great-Grandma would make it out of the hospital, but for those couple hours, we were our family unit of four. We cherished every minute we had.

The goodbye was hard, especially for the kids. They cried like I haven't heard them cry before. As we made the drive home along Highway 40, my daughter, in the midst of her tears, sniffled as she looked out the left window. There was a rainbow! She turned to her brother and said, "That rainbow is God's way of telling us it's going to be okay, and He will care for us and reunite us with Daddy soon." How amazing it is to see that children can find symbols and signs in the simplest of things. That moment was special for me because it showed me the importance of being present, even in sad situations.

My daughter was right – it's important to see and feel all of your environment because you may be able to find your strength in doing so. Yes, my daughter was sad, but she didn't let her sadness overtake her to the point of not noticing the beauty of that rainbow. That's a lesson in itself. However, that's not all that happened in this moment. I too, was practicing my ability to be present, and as a result, I was able to hear this exchange, which ultimately gave me strength. There's another lesson. My daughter's presence influenced and strengthened me as well. That's a testament to how our presence or lack thereof can affect those around us. Whew! All of that came just from a car-ride and the fact that I was present enough in the moment to see it. That's why being present is so important. There is so much clarity and knowledge to be gained when you are present and aware of all that is around you. Even when things seem like they are falling apart, make it a point to be present. You might be surprised at the benefits of doing so.

Another lesson I've learned from being present with my children is that someone is always watching. You may not always be aware of it, but you are being watched – by your kids, your friends, and colleagues. What are they going to see in your life?

My daughter plays softball, and recently, there weren't enough girls to make a team. Consequently, the coaches asked her if she wanted to join the boys team. Without hesitation she said, "Momma, you are the only girl on your work calls, and I want to be brave just like you. I want to play with the boys, and it's ok that I'm the solo girl on the baseball team." That comment hit me between the eyes like David's pebble hit Goliath. Sometimes we need to keep our ears and hearts open, even to the smallest of tiny humans. What I realized was that she was watching. She was listening. She was observing. She was absorbing and taking bits and pieces of what she witnessed in my life and adapting them to her own life and experiences.

Being present requires intentional awareness, and one way to be intentionally aware is to be an active listener. What does being an active listener mean? It's when you set intentions to hear the words, the purpose of the message, and the context surrounding it all. MindTools shares the following reasons that we listen:

- We listen to obtain information
- We listen to understand
- We listen for enjoyment
- We listen to learn

Are you practicing and modeling active listening in your conversations and behavior? What if you were to make a conscious effort to be present with active listening? How could it transform your GSD Factor life?

Throughout history many cultures have shown that the family unit is meant to include multiple generations under one roof or within a community. We, as adults, overthink things. We know all the scenarios where things could go well or bad, and, at times, that taints our viewpoint. What if we were able to dream big again? What if we were able to see life through the eyes of a child? What if we listened to them? What if we didn't dismiss their views or perspectives?

This applies to our professional lives as well. How many emails or instant chat messages could be saved if we slowed down to truly read or listen to what is being said? How many meetings about meetings about meetings could be reduced if we got rid of distractions, were present with one another, respected the viewpoints given, and truly heard before speaking or sending that email?

I have one client who is a stickler about eyes and faces up, being engaged and not multitasking during meetings. She established a fine system. She set up a digital cash account and had a jar in the office. If you weren't paying attention, you had to pay the fine for lack of engagement. You know what? It worked. Suddenly, meetings were more productive because everyone was engaged, present, and able to GSD much more quickly.

Let these lessons resonate throughout your life. We are all works in progress, me included. I encourage you to be present. To slow down. To listen and to hear and to open yourself to hearing messages in places and from people from whom you might not expect them. You will be amazed at the fulfillment and abundance it brings to life.

GSD moment of reflection

Answer these prompts in the space below or on the GSD Factor Hub:

Are you present? What headwinds are standing in the way and not allowing you to be present?

_____

_____

_____

Do you actually slow down to hear your family? Friends? Colleagues? Those that you consider to be part of your Clan or Insiders Board?

_____

_____

_____

Are you modeling the best behavior? What behavior would you want to consider evolving or transforming?

_____

_____

_____

www.gsdfactor.com

A SPACE TO DREAM BIG . . .

A SPACE TO DREAM BIG . . .

⅂

PIVOT DECISIONS

Red pill or blue pill?

My earliest memory of having to make a pivot decision, a decision which completely changed the trajectory of my life, started at the age of sixteen. I was on my way to a professional dance career with our ballet company, training with some amazing dancers that would go on to the likes of Juilliard, Alvin Ailey, and Boston Conservatory. As the youngest member of the junior company by two years, my path was already taking a slightly different direction because of school, but my instructors, parents and I had a plan to graduate early to open the way for me to go to the Royal Ballet of Canada. Then I got sick, very sick. For two years I didn't know what was wrong, but all of a sudden, my body and brain could no longer do the things that I had been trained to do. They wouldn't listen to the commands and muscle memory. After that long stretch of the unknown and uncertainty, countless tests and doctors all over the South and Midwest, I was finally diagnosed with Lyme's disease. At this time, the research surrounding Lyme's disease was relatively new, and there wasn't much known about this debilitating, even life-threatening, disease. At the time of diagnosis, doctors gave me less than three months to live. My focus in life was no longer ballet training in the studio for six plus hours per day, but in just trying to walk or swim in the pool. My focus was no longer on studying like crazy trying to complete high school earlier to pursue my ballet career, but rather, on pivoting to figure out if I was going to live, what my career and passion would be now.

After being diagnosed with Lyme's disease, I was quickly shifted from the pre-professional homeschool life familiar to many gymnasts and dancers. That's what the sport called for, but I now had to get accustomed to what I would classify as a normal life. What was this thing called high school? I wasn't sure, but I decided to fully embrace my junior and senior year by taking advanced classes, being elected as a class officer, enrolling in the theater program, volunteering with the younger students, and contributing to year end book projects. Whatever school had to offer, I was there for it.

Once my Lyme's disease was fully in remission after two years of treatments, I was ready for my next pivot as I've mentioned before of co-founding a dance school. Some pivots in life present multiple lessons and nuggets and it's important to lean in. Just a year after opening up the dance school where I was feeding my love of dance by teaching and choreographing, life threw another curve ball at me. This one would require me to have four knee surgeries over the course of eighteen months. Are you kidding me? I had lost dance once. I pivoted my dream to teaching and choreography, got back into dance shape and was performing with my students, which was such an honor. And for what? For it to be taken again? I didn't want to dream again. I didn't want to reinvent myself again. Now I was faced with countless hours of physical therapy and training to learn to walk again. Dance was no longer an option. Timing was forcing me to look for a new passion and pursuit.

My late father had always said I had to have a backup plan, just in case. He was a two-time Rose Bowl QB winner with Stanford University, but he also experienced countless injuries, which didn't allow for his professional career. Consequently, he pivoted to the Air Force. Knowing my dad's journey and pivots taught me that no matter what life throws at you, you *can* pivot. You can find the next thing that brings you joy, peace, satisfaction, and fulfillment.

For many years, I had to find other outlets besides dance, and one of those outlets turned out to be coaching people. I love dreaming big with them. I love getting in a room and white boarding out themes, concepts, and words and then seeing how it all ties together. I live for the text message or call that says, "I have a problem. Can we chat?" I'm here for the good, bad, and tricky situations because we are dealing with different types of personalities, cultures and team dynamics. I get joy from putting words to people's plans or journey mapping in action. I love when I can team up with someone and walk out of those sessions. It feels good to know that I helped someone do something amazing, or given them key actions, steps and a plan for what to do next. It's like a puzzle. You can either start at all the edges and move in, or start by finding the individual themes within and grouping it. You can approach it anyway you want or the best way for your brain, but the ultimate goal is to finish the puzzle. I like being there to help put that puzzle together. If those circumstances with my health and my injuries hadn't happened, I would not be sitting where I am today. You would not be reading this book. Those events, and how I allowed them to mold and shape me, opened up opportunities for the future.

There are times in everyone's life when we come to a decision point or crossroads where it is clear that there are two paths, two choices, red pill or blue pill? Those are the pivot moments that can lead to reinvention and a whole different set of opportunities. These decisions can be scary because of the uncertainty, but they can also be hugely profitable and impactful if navigated effectively. We don't have to look that far for examples. One of my favorite types of pivots surrounds women athletes after their sports careers have ended. Serena Williams and Allyson Felix have both transitioned their successful sports careers of tennis and track and field, respectively into highly successful careers in fashion, which is different from the typical athlete-to-coach transition. I'm also interested in entertainers who use their celebrity status to transition into other sectors. Matthew McConaughey, for instance, has used his successful acting career to pivot into activism including a partnership with Salesforce.com to serve as a brand ambassador and advisor for their new Team Earth campaign. Another good example is Reese Witherspoon who has leveraged her influence in the entertainment industry to create her own production company, which she eventually sold for over 900 million dollars. Talk about a successful pivot! These are only a few high-profile examples of successful pivots, but there are countless examples of people who have had to make leaps into new opportunities. They all had to answer difficult questions to do so. Should I go left or go right? Should I push forward, or should I stop? Should I remain satisfied, or keep pushing?

Where was the point in your career, job or project when you knew it was time to pivot or move on to something else? It happens to all of us at some point or the other. For me, it came after the knee injury. I realized that the damage of the knee injury compounded with the after-effects of Lyme's disease had made my career in dance all but impossible. During my recovery process, I began to accept that and began a more focused career in business. There is a fine line between leaving on your own terms, leaving at a natural transition point, or leaving knowing you are leaving your client, project, or company in a hole. Sometimes you have control over the circumstances of your pivot, and other times you don't, but the way in which you handle the transition is always up to you.

I've had a number of pivots in my life that I've shared throughout this book: from leaving the dance world, to leaving corporate America for the pursuits of entrepreneurship. There's never the perfect time; however, there is a right time and, definitely, a wrong time. I don't believe in there being a perfect time because every transition should have an element of risk or uncertainty. None of us know for certain whether the move will be successful. However, for me, the "right time" is when I stop feeling challenged by my current role or when my views and beliefs no longer align with the company's. Whatever the nature of the transition, there are a couple of pointers or things to keep in mind that have guided me over the course of my career surrounding transitions or evolving.

What does pivoting look like in a career? Let's say that you've made it through interviews and onboarding for a new job that you believe is your dream job, but you are a few months in and suddenly don't feel like this is the right fit. It is natural and expected to do an evaluation at the ninety-day mark. Establish early on with your boss that you would like regular check-ins within the first ninety days to ensure that you are meeting their expectations. This also gives you the backing and support that you need in case something changes for you. It usually takes a good ninety days to really figure out if something is going to work out or not.

If you are within your ninety-day window, approach your boss and outline reasons why you don't think this is working out, but assure him/her that you will see your notice out and participate in any knowledge transfer to minimize impact.

If you are past your ninety-day window and realize that it's time for that pivot, then evaluate your situation and conduct a self-inventory to help with your decision. Are you being physically, emotionally or verbally injured? Is the situation toxic? How is your mental health? Is the situation causing physical stress to your body? If you answer yes to any of these questions, you need to exit quickly because no job is worth losing your health. This is one of the many reasons I decided to pivot into entrepreneurship. I realized that the best chance of me truly achieving work-life-family integration would only come if I had the autonomy to dictate my own schedule and make my own decisions about the projects and clients I take.

I also decided to go into entrepreneurship because I wanted to be my own boss, and I wanted to provide a safe space for other people to work. I want to be a company that keeps operations low so that our contractors can run their business through ours and still make a reasonable profit for themselves.

The next tip is applicable if your reasons for leaving are because you don't agree with how business is being handled or decision-making doesn't align with your core personal or professional beliefs. When that happens, you must be cautious that you don't stay there too long. Don't be complacent. Don't get comfortable. Force the change. Change is healthy. If you are in this boat, mild frustration can quickly escalate and turn into resentment and bitterness, which will come across in your demeanor, work encounters, and your work deliverables. Begin to look for a good transition exit strategy so that you don't leave those left behind in too much of a pickle.

Whenever you do exit, you want to do your best not to burn bridges because depending on industry or function, you could be in tight circles, and word could travel fast. If the situation is less than optimal, leave quickly, sooner rather than later, and as you are interviewing for the next opportunity, be transparent and honest about your circumstances.

It is extremely rare nowadays that anyone will remain in one position or at one company for the entirety of their career. As a matter of fact, some studies have even stated that millennials will most likely have about thirteen jobs in their lifetime. The need to pivot is almost inevitable, and it doesn't have to be a bad thing. Just try to keep the aforementioned tips in mind as you are making the best decision for you.

GSD moment of reflection

Answer these prompts in the space below or on the GSD Factor Hub:

What pivot have you experienced in your life?

_____

_____

_____

Is there a pivot that you need to prepare for?

_____

_____

_____

Have you dreamed big about what your post pivot person looks like or is doing?

_____

_____

_____

www.gsdfactor.com

A SPACE TO DREAM BIG . . .

ACTION PLAN
FOR BEING PRESENT

Being present may seem like a more passive GSD attribute, but the reality is that being present involves a great deal of intentionality. Think about it. All of the sub attributes in this section require constant consideration and adjustment of our perception. You cannot keep showing up; focusing on progress, not perfection; being present; or make pivot decisions if you are not consistently and intentionally thinking of doing all those things. The hardest part about consistently and intentionally being present by maintaining all four of these sub attributes is the risk of falling into perfectionism. If you find that you lean on the side of perfectionism, or you are a recovering perfectionist, here are some actionable steps you can take to be present without being a perfectionist.

1. Keep showing up. Create a list of small, go-to steps that will ensure you keep showing up which means being present, even if for a moment. It's the art of doing something – anything, and trusting that process, even when it seems that there are more pivots than plans. Your small steps can include things like a daily gratitude journal or a check-in with a work-out partner. Whatever the steps are, they will be unique to your lifestyle and should be tailored to whatever you need to keep you in a state of awareness to keep showing up.

2. Extend yourself grace. This is more of an informal step, but it's still important. Make sure you are reminding yourself that the focus is progress not perfection and that, therefore, you will mess up. You will make mistakes. The key is to accept wherever you are in your process, so that it's easier for you to commit to taking a step, any step, forward.

3. Celebrate your wins. As a recovering perfectionist, I now appreciate the fact that progress is good enough. Moving the needle, accomplishing one task, or doing one thing for ourselves should be celebrated. Take the time to do that. It can be as small as a verbal, "Good job" to yourself, or as big as throwing a party when you reach your goals. Whatever the accomplishment, acknowledge it and celebrate it.

The commitment to being present requires a change in mindset, reminding us to be actively aware of tapes that are rolling our heads, and when our minds wander, we must reset, be it with meditation, music, or spoken word. Being present also means remembering the simplest of things – to breathe. I have a picture on my desk of two beautifully painted lungs that simply says, "Inhale, exhale." Bring it back to your breath. It will bring clarity. It will slow down your heart rate. It will steady the emotions and nerves. Finally, being present requires an ever-present attitude of gratitude for progress and not perfection. It's great to get all the things done, but this attribute allows you to be grateful and accepting of the times when you don't.

Visit www.gsdfactor.com to join our GSD Factor Hub where you can take the Be Present assessment that will provide prescriptive recommendations based on where you want to ignite presence in your life.

ATTRIBUTE FIVE

BE **RESILIENT**

The choice to persevere, to activate stamina and grit, and to acknowledge that life can be shit, but we must learn, grow and turn the negatives into positives.

66

Hardships often prepare ordinary people for an extraordinary destiny.

—C.S. Lewis

99

RESILIENT LIFE

Throughout this book, I've talked about the power of showing up, trying and failing quickly and trying again, pivoting, and learning something from every situation. All these lessons are driving towards the GSD Factor attribute of being resilient.

Being resilient is about having an attitude that says life can be shitty with days that are good and days that are bad, but the sun rises in the morning. Resilience requires honest acknowledgment of where you are. In order to be resilient, you have to be authentic with yourself and your current circumstances.

The late Jane Marczewski knew resilience and openly shared the importance of keeping that positive mindset. A singer-songwriter from Zanesville, Ohio, you may have known her as Nightbirde from her time competing on *America's Got Talent (AGT)* in 2021. She had actually been performing and writing songs for almost her whole life before she ever got to the show. She even opened for Tori Kelly once, but it was her amazing and heart-felt performance of her original song, *It's OK* on her AGT audition that catapulted her into the spotlight. She received Simon Cowell's Golden Buzzer for that performance and immediately became a favorite of the show.

In addition to being a talented pop-folk performer and songwriter, Nightbirde was also a cancer patient, having been declared cancer free twice to only find herself battling for her life again. Her poetry, music, and spoken word was real. It was raw and authentic. She lived a beautiful expression of resilience. While talking to the AGT judges, she said what became one of my favorite quotes from her. The judges asked her if she was okay because she had just revealed that she still had traces of cancer in her spine, lungs and liver, and it was obvious that they were all starting to feel sorry for her. She confidently replied: "It's important that everyone knows that I'm so much more than the bad things that happen to me... You can't wait until life isn't hard anymore before you decide to be happy." Whew! If that's not resilience, I don't know what is!

She was living out the GSD Factor life. This woman was actively battling terminal cancer with a two percent chance of survival and still found the energy to follow her dreams and passion. Eventually, her health took a downward turn, and she made the decision to leave the show to focus on recovery. Even then, however, she would take to Instagram to share encouragement and motivation with others, while clearly going through some of the hardest days of her life. What was particularly inspiring to see was how she never sugarcoated her experience. Oftentimes, she would let people know that her days and treatments were difficult, but she showed resilience by not letting it stop her from living. She was still writing, still creating music, and still helping others, through all of that.

Sadly, Nightbirde lost her battle with cancer almost one year after appearing on AGT. I'm sad that I never got a chance to meet her because I would have loved to have hosted her on the GSD Factor Podcast. Our stories of our health had some similarities, which is why it resonates so deeply with me. I know what it feels like to have health issues that prevent you from being able to live out your dreams. Her resilience looked different than mine, yet I found encouragement and comfort in her story, in her songs, in her words. Soon after her death, her family shared one of her videos with the world in which she stated: "Just because you're sad or grieving doesn't mean you're not grateful, doesn't mean you're not hopeful…But sadness and grief and mourning and lamenting and crying and screaming and being angry, these are the ways that we honor what was lost." What a true statement, to which I would add that part of being resilient is knowing that when you are knocked down, it's okay to sit, cry, yell, scream, or do whatever you need to do in that moment. Those feelings need to get out. We are human, and we all feel things. That's how we were created. Resilience is not pushing down those feelings of sadness or anger but holding them, honoring them and then letting them go. We hold space for them for as long as they still serve us. We are present with them as long as it takes to get it out of our system. That's what you need, but then, you rise from the ashes. You get back up.

Think about a loss you have experienced in your life or a traumatic event or situation that robbed you of something? Have you given yourself permission to grieve it? Have you even talked about it? I have found, in these moments, that the sooner I talk, cry, yell or scream out my frustrations, the sooner my head, heart, and emotions all come back into alignment to be present in that moment and face the grief, sorrow, anger, and injustice head-on so that I could honor what I had been through but also prepare for the better things ahead. One such moment came when I found out my daughter was being bullied at school. I'll get into more detail about what happened later, but the moment I found out, I went into full-blown emotional roller-coaster status. I was sad, angry and scared, and it all came out in the form of tears. It was ugly, but I needed to get all of that out before I talked to my daughter and before I talked to anybody at that school.

As for the details of the story and with many situations in life, my kids have taught me some of the best lessons in resilience. It's often said that kids are most resilient because they are quick to forgive and let go. Thank you, *Frozen*, for that life-long lesson! My daughter taught me and my family about true resilience after surviving various forms of bullying at school. For the better part of a year, it was verbal, and we would coach our daughter on the "sassy" words spoken to her. We would acknowledge that they were unkind and that they were hurtful. We would talk it out, paint it out, or even act it out. Then, we would role-play and practice what we could say back to show our strength and confidence. We talked about being resilient, building a thick skin, ducking it out by staying calm on the surface.

One year, the school was to host a father-daughter dance, and she was so excited. I told her she needed to start to think about what she wanted to wear, and she said, "I already know! Daddy and I are going to go in our matching Nashville Predators hockey jerseys." They both love the team. They go to games, and after all, there was no specific attire required. We, as parents, had a choice to make. Should we allow her to conform to the way things normally are at these types of events, or let her be her own person? We knew that if they did wear these non-traditional school dance clothes, they would get comments, but we prepared her and gave her a choice. She was unwavering. This was her, and this was what her heart desired. Congratulating her for being confident in herself, leaning into her unicorn, and voicing what she wanted, we sat her down and said, "Yes, absolutely, but just know that that is not the usual attire for these types of things. Daddy is all in and here for it. We just want you to know that some people may stare, and some people may say something. We will prepare and coach you on how you can respond." Her response: "Let's do it!"

Sure enough, they showed up to all the dads wearing black suits and all the girls wearing dresses. She looked up at her daddy as they walked in and said, "Everyone is going to see us. They will know that I love the Nashville Predators, and so do you. This is who we are! I'm so excited!" Then, with her little giggle, she said,

"Besides we are eating pizza, and I think we look way more comfortable than everyone else!"

Of course, it went as expected. That night, sure enough, some people commented how awesome it was and were so impressed by her authenticity, courage and boldness to be herself. Some others thought it was uncool and not okay that she didn't wear what little girls are "supposed to" wear at dances. She broke the unspoken rules. She didn't look fancy enough to them, but she did not flinch. My daughter was ready and coached and would politely say, "Thank you. This is me. This is my favorite team, and my Dad and I are HUGE fans. We even go to games together!" She remembered her coaching; she remembered the role-play practice and was able to respond respectfully but unapologetically. Her literal mind loved responding with things like, "How can I break any rules around what to wear when there weren't any dress code rules written in the invitation?" My favorite of my daughter's responses was when she told her bullies, as they were eating their pizza dinner, "It's a lot easier to eat pizza in hockey clothes than it is in a fancy dress." She had a blast that night, front and center on the dance floor. You couldn't miss her wearing her Nashville Predators gold jersey, loud and proud. As parents, we couldn't have been more proud of the lifelong lessons that were learned that night.

When she got home and shared what had gone on, I checked that she didn't need to cry or get angry about the unkind things said, and she said, "No, Mom. Remember, I'm strong, brave, beautiful, and resilient. I've got this. You taught me how."

Unfortunately, things escalated sometime after this. The bully was first attempting to socially ostracize our daughter by creating exclusive clubs and trying to make our daughter "audition" to join. Our daughter, being the unicorn that she is, refused to humor the bully and simply decided that she just wouldn't be a part, so then the bully continued to make snide remarks and comments about our daughter. Yes, confidence and uniqueness can be taught at a young age, but so can insecurity and fear of people and things that are different. My daughter's boldness and authenticity seemed to threaten the bully, and once the bully figured out that their words were having no effect on our daughter, they did what most bullies do. The bully resorted to physical harm, and our daughter got hurt. She cried, and we cried with her. She was angry, and trust me, we were angry with her. We talked about it a lot with her therapist, her coaches, her priest, you name it. Talking about it acknowledged that it happened. It helped process the grief and anger experienced. My own way of processing was writing and communicating to all parties, including school administration, education boards, etc.

Soon after the situation occurred, we started talking to our daughter about the importance of acknowledging that it happens. We taught her that it is important to give herself time to heal from the hurt inflicted by others and to work towards forgiveness, even if the other party doesn't extend it. Now this does not mean seeking reconciliation, because there are times that face-to-face forgiveness and reconciliation are not physically safe choices. However, seeking forgiveness, in your own heart, is necessary to free yourself.

Remember GSDers, your kids are watching. Your teammates are watching. Your bully or harasser is watching. We knew that when we started escalating and fighting for our daughter's safety in school that we were being watched. As we communicated, we were factual and made clear our intentions. We wanted to protect our daughter first and foremost. We were also concerned about the other child because obviously this behavior was learned some way and carries implications about the home life of that child. Finally, what policies or procedures needed to be improved so that our situation didn't happen again to another child? Where could we bring about change? In what tone or voice would we propose changes? How could we demonstrate resilience to our daughter, demonstrate forgiveness and demonstrate how we could take something intended for the negative and transform it into a positive?

We were heard. Our thoughtful and mindful approach brought about much needed awareness and training around bullying in the schools and other umbrella programs. The school implemented more training and strategies to recognize and address bullying for the faculty, staff, and students. There was also a system-wide initiative to increase training and awareness for bullying throughout all the schools in the county. Just the other day, I walked into the office and saw no-less than four anti-bullying posters on the walls in the school, which were not there before this incident. In a way, all of these changes were part of our healing because, yes, this awful thing happened, but we channeled that to bring about change. We turned that negative into a positive. It was also an empowering growth opportunity for our daughter. This was helped, in part, through her workbook and exercises provided by the nonprofit organization, Hello Bloom, whose goal is to support and encourage girls to grow after they have experienced bullying through their social-emotional learning program. It was through this program that our daughter found her voice and wanted to share her story with others. She hoped that by sharing her story, bullies would become aware of their actions and that they would learn to be kind. She hoped that by sharing her story with others that had walked similar paths that they would not feel alone, but feel hopeful, stronger, and more confident.

Those that are extremely resilient take it one step further. Resilience can look different in many ways. It can look like not backing down on your principles or creating awareness and advocacy. Throughout history we have seen hero after hero demonstrate resilience – people like Amy Purdy, a double amputee who lost her legs after a bout with meningitis but then showed resilience by learning to live with prosthetic legs and winning a bronze medal in snowboarding in the 2014 Winter Paralympics. Then there's people like Malala Yousafzai, a Pakistani education activist who was shot on a school bus by a member of the Taliban for speaking publicly on behalf of girls' right to education and equality. Did she stop? No. She continues to advocate for girls' right to education in her country, and as a result became the youngest person ever to receive the Nobel Peace Prize.

Nightbirde, Amy, and Malala all share the gift of resiliency. They are shining examples of what leading a resilient life means. Being resilient is about pushing through obstacles, standing up, and sharing personal stories of triumph over adversity. It's saying enough is enough. It's staying in your country with your citizens during an invasion and war. It's also collective movements like that of the US female soccer team using their success and platform to bring about change in the equal pay movement. It's asking questions like, "What can I do to make this better? What can I do to bring about change? What can I do to bring about awareness?" It's not just overcoming and bouncing back from setbacks in my own life. It's also figuring out how to use my life and my triumphs to help somebody else.

Another one of my favorite quotes from Nightbirde is: "Life is a game of choosing your pain – the pain of continuing or the pain of giving up. The pain of continuing has a lot more uncertainties, but the pain of giving up is so much worse." How many of us have perhaps chosen the pain of giving up? Maybe you were bullied in school, but the adults around you didn't listen and hear you. Perhaps you were harassed at work. You never grieved what was lost, and you couldn't find the path continuing with pain.

There's good news. It's not too late to change your path of giving up to the path of continuing. It's not too late for you to reach a place of forgiveness, even if it's not reciprocated. It's not too late for you to evaluate your healing journey and say this event can make me more resilient for the next time. Maybe if people hear my own story, they will be able to ignite the fire of resiliency in their own lives.

Athletes are some of the best examples of resilience. They often reflect on losses and wins. They study footage and tape to see what they did wrong, so they can learn and not make the same mistake again. In business we call this process "retrospect." It's during this time that we ask the tough questions. What went wrong? What could we have done better, and what can we do better moving forward?

Applying the process of retrospecting to life will reveal that we never reach a finished level of resilient life. We are all works in progress. Resilience is one of those things upon which we can continue to grow and improve. It's one of the first lessons we learn when we are born, and it can be one of the final lessons before you move on from this life. Each day can be a lesson in resilience. Each time you find yourself in a circumstance asking, "What can I learn from this? What can I learn to do versus not to do," that's you exercising your resilience muscle. That's how you grow and expand your resilience and stamina. The next time something comes up, an experience with bullying, a life-threatening illness, a divorce, whatever it is, your resilience muscle memory will kick in, and it will become a little easier to bounce back. Being resilient is the GSD Factor attribute and life skill of knowing that even though we have to go through things in life, we can learn something, and we can help somebody else by sharing that lesson. As we are walking out that journey, it is becoming a part of our story. A story that can be shared with others. A story that brings change. A story that brings hope.

GSD moment of reflection

Answer these prompts in the space below or on the GSD Factor Hub:

What resilience moments have you experienced in your life?

_____

_____

_____

In what experience do you wish you had exercised more resilience?

_____

_____

_____

"I _____ (insert name here) am resilient. I matter. I am a force to be reckoned with. I love myself. I am bold. I am brave. I am brilliant. My voice is my strongest weapon." Now how does that quote make you feel?

_____

_____

_____

A SPACE TO DREAM BIG . . .

A SPACE TO DREAM BIG . . .

TRUST THE TIMING

Much of what we've discussed as it pertains to the GSD Factor attributes and sub attributes has been dependent on parts of our lives that we can control. You can control how you show up in the world by being confident. You can control how much you know by being inquisitive. You can control how you handle problems by being imaginative and how you react to life's curveballs by being present. Being resilient also has an element of personal control in that you have to make a choice to continue to get up after being knocked down, but there is an element of uncertainty that exists within this GSD Factor attribute that doesn't necessarily show up in others. Timing. No matter how confident, inquisitive, imaginative or present we are in any situation, if the timing isn't right, it's not happening. That's what makes resilience so important and sometimes challenging. Being resilient also means being aware that we cannot control timing, but we must trust it.

What does it look like to trust the timing? Though we can't control timing, we aren't just passively experiencing time. However, before we can jump into how we must trust the timing, let's talk about how we manage the time we have. I'm someone who easily has thirty hours of work each day, and since there are only twenty-four hours in a day, I've had to learn to organize and prioritize. It can be easy to give up things like self-care and sleep, but as some-one who is a recovering work-aholic and burn-out survivor, I can attest to the fact that sacrificing self-care for anything else is not worth it.

You have to take care of yourself first. Consider this: what we give to others comes from what we give to ourselves. Furthermore, if we haven't made time to give ourselves rest, love, grace, patience, etc., where are we going to find it to give to others? Your family, your team, your organization, and *you* are all counting on you. If you aren't able to be there, those things don't function the way they are intended to. Now, that doesn't mean that you can't ever not be there. It means that if you are not there, it should not be as a result of your lack of self-care. Managing our time to include self-care requires balance. That's the real issue. Remember we are striving for work-life-family integration and that includes self-care.

When you evaluate your workload, think about what progress, not perfection, looks like.

I'm always evaluating what needs to be done, and I always have a list. One of my project managers shared that she categorizes her personal and professional life into three buckets:

Now – These are the items that are immediate, today maybe tomorrow, but it is critical to getting done.

Next – These are the items that may be completed tomor-row or this week. They are a close follower after the now items but aren't the most pressing.

Later – These are the items that can have a little more time to ideate and plan. They could be addressed next week, next month or quarter, etc.

However you decide to group your long to-do list, and what-ever timing buckets you use, just know that it doesn't all have to be done today. It can't all be done by you. Ask for help. Along with admitting that I'm not the smartest person in the room, by knowing how to pull a team into GSD, I also remind myself that I'm not expected to get it all done. Thankfully, I've been blessed with an amazing team that I can mobilize and delegate, and, together, we GSD. I will be the first to tell you that even I have not perfected this, but, again, we are all works in progress. We must extend ourselves grace in those moments.

Establishing standard operation processes, even when you are a company of one, is super critical for your time-saving and consistent execution. Build yourself some templates that you can plug and play or that you can then share with a virtual assistant (VA) to rinse and repeat. I had never considered a VA before until I realized that my team and I were spending considerable time doing things that were important, but that could be done by someone else. My team and I needed to focus on tasks that were more specialized and specific to the company's needs, like corresponding with clients about their specific projects. We needed to delegate general administrative tasks like managing schedules, checking the general emails and direct messages, and other day-to-day operations to another party. I reached out to a VA company whose founder I knew to ask if their VAs had this skillset, which they did. It wasn't until I heard all their capabilities and offerings that I started to see the opportunity for me to offload a number of tasks that were important, but no longer required my limited and valuable time. Be willing to explore options; be willing to listen and hear people that want to help. Be humble enough to realize that other people are capable of doing some of the things that you think only you can do. They may even be better at those things than you, and that's okay! Do not be afraid to get help. Whether it's in your personal life or professional life, if you have the resources to enlist help, I encourage you to do so. Yes, you can get shit done alone, but you can really get shit done when you've got help!

I know what you're thinking. Time management is great. Getting help is awesome, but what happens when life starts throwing curveballs? Well, that's when we get to start trusting the timing. Athletes and dancers have an incredible sense of timing – timing of movements, timing of breathing, timing of sequence. As the daughter of a quarterback, I was raised watching film and routes of quarterbacks and receivers. Reading the defense in football is much like reacting to the challenges and uncertainties of life. Sure, there may be a plan, but maybe life is throwing us something for which we weren't prepared, forcing us to call an audible. An audible is a football term for when the quarterback suspects that the defense is changing up their strategy and changes the play. The quarterback has already given the offense a play in the huddle, but right before it's time to execute, the quarterback senses a shift in the defense's strategy. As a result, he or she makes an executive decision to change plays to face this new strategy. That happens all the time in real life. We make plans as well as we can, and suddenly life shifts those plans. Then, like quarterbacks, we have to pause, re-evaluate, and re-execute.

In keeping with the football analogy, I can say that throughout my life, there have been many instances where the defense blitzed, causing me to call an audible. In some cases, I had to pause, re-evaluate, and re-execute. Life has taught me the importance of being agile. By looking at the past, retrospectively, I can see how it prepared me for the future. Get good with change. Change is healthy. Change means that you are growing and evolving.

When you are thinking through strategic timing you must have a vision that is fueling that passion. That vision is your steadfast. Even when the timing seems off or the strategy needs to be changed, your vision remains. Part of having that solid vision is having that foundation early on of knowing who you are and what you want out of life. That is your compass. That is your constant.

I remember going through a really rough patch with one of my companies. We had a great pipeline, and with its execution we were going to be able to bring on multiple full-time team members. I was excited. My team was excited. My family was excited. Mostly every opportunity was in the final proposal and or contract stage. Then, in one day, five opportunities died. Pretty soon, each one of the remaining opportunities died as well. We couldn't move the rest of the pipeline along fast enough to fill the void that had been created. I was so disappointed, and I was mad. I started to question my vision and in turn my why. I started to doubt myself. Why was I, all of a sudden, being rejected? We have talked about the concept that sometimes the rejection or the no is because there is something better coming.

What I didn't know then was that I was being prepared for some of the biggest opportunities to come down the pike. Because we weren't bogged down with smaller contracts and clients, we were allowed to sharpen our skills, improve our standard operating processes, and refine our value proposition, so when those bigger-fish opportunities started to come our way, we were ready. In this case, the bigger opportunity was securing a year-long contract with a global company on a digital transformation that touched countries around the world. It also allowed me the opportunity to finish this book that you are reading right now. We were slowed down, so that we could speed up to succeed and ultimately achieve scalable growth.

As I always say, we can learn something from every opportunity. We can learn what to do and what not to do. With each prospect or opportunity that flows in and out, we ask ourselves, "What did we learn? What can we carry with us for future growth? From what were we being protected? I'm not saying you won't be disappointed or need to be reminded to keep your chin up, but this healthy outlook makes the rejections a little easier to swallow and puts you into the positive mindset, the GSD Factor mindset.

You hear of stories of successful people around the world that made money, then went bankrupt, only to rise to the top again. Precious Williams, a thirteen-time national elevator pitch competition winner and founder of Perfect Pitches by Precious is a perfect example of such a journey. After a successful appearance on Shark Tank, she secured funding for her first business Curvy Girls Lingerie. She was doing really well when she experienced the loss of a loved one, fell into alcoholism, and lost everything. However, her resilience and ability to trust the timing helped her rebuild a brand-new empire, and she's now a nationally known corporate trainer, motivational speaker and successful author of *Bad Bitches and Power Pitches*. Precious's life shows us that you can plan and even experience success, but then life can hit you with the unexpected and turn your world upside down. That's when you have to flex that resilience muscle. I love stories like Precious's. It shows that resilience and trusting the timing go hand in hand. She didn't know when things were going to turn around for her, but she kept trying and didn't give up even after such great losses. She didn't know that one of the lowest moments in her life would be the fertilizing ground for the growth of her next venture. People like that inspire me because during their dark time, they don't lose sight of their vision. This is where the attribute of showing up comes back into play. They just kept walking through the timing because, maybe, it would lead to other things and become a strategic move.

Perhaps another lesson to be learned from trusting the timing is whether your vision can stand the pressure of the seasons of uncertainty. Can your vision stand the test of time? Can it stand adversity? Can it stand the failures and successes? When timing and vision are being challenged or refined, that is a great opportunity to determine whether you should do or be. Ask yourself, "Do I need to push or pull during this period?" Only you truly know what you need as you are walking out your story and your journey.

Trusting the timing is an important part of this attribute, because it also requires you to trust yourself. You have to trust in your own management of the time you have been given and trust that you have prepared as much as you possibly can for those unexpected twists and turns of life. No matter how many times you get knocked down, trust the timing. Trust yourself and get back up. Eventually, you'll walk right into your success.

GSD moment of reflection

Answer these prompts in the space below or on the GSD Factor Hub:

What timing story have you experienced in your own life?

_____

_____

_____

If you were rejected by someone or something, did it turn out to be for your protection?

_____

_____

_____

Is there something you are walking through right now that is causing you to trust the timing?

_____

_____

_____

www.gsdfactor.com

A SPACE TO DREAM BIG . . .

A SPACE TO DREAM BIG . . .

PERSPECTIVE

Have you ever met or known someone whose presence can brighten up a difficult situation just by offering a different view? I call them "breath-of-fresh-air" people. These people provide balance by providing another way to look at things. I've had the pleasure of working with a few people like this.

One of them was a project manager for one of my recent client engagements. She was such a joy to work with because I didn't have to walk on eggshells around her. Her personality was a great balance to mine. She was strong, yet calm and unassuming. She definitely knew how to get shit done, but she had different ways of doing and saying things that balanced out my boldness and intensity. Whenever we would have a difficult problem or challenge, she often gave insight that I or others hadn't thought of. She was a great advocate and sounding board, and working with her showed me two valuable things. One was that women can definitely have positive working relationships, void of competition and imposter syndrome. The other revelation I had was that these types of people bring a refreshing outlook to situations because of one main thing – perspective.

Perspective is the way we see life and the experiences it brings. Being faced with the daily battle of just living can bring perspective like nothing else. Fighting to live cuts through the shit and forces you to see and acknowledge what truly matters.

Ask anyone who has been faced with significant obstacles and forced to be grateful for the small things such as breathing, eating, or walking about their perspective. Their perseverance. I've shared my experience with my life-threatening illness of Lyme's disease. Before I was officially diagnosed with Lyme's Disease, one of the biggest challenges wasn't all my physical struggles; it was the mental difficulties because doctors couldn't figure out what was wrong. There was a period of time where a diagnosis or a test would not give them the answer. Their science deduced that it was all in my head.

When I finally heard the diagnosis from the single Lyme's disease specialist here in the states who was world-renowned in his cutting-edge research and treatments, I experienced a wave of relief in knowing that I had found my answer at last. Though I now had the mental struggle of accepting that life as I knew it was about to be drastically different, there was some solace in knowing that my sickness was not a figment of my imagination. There was extreme psychological stress around adjusting my schedule to fill all the hours that used to be filled with dance and to reimagine what my future looked like without being a professional dancer. However, there was a perspective lesson to be learned – the value of having a supportive family. My family supported and loved me through the whole traumatic ordeal. My parents fought, pushed, and looked for answers. My sister showed up. She would help me get into the pool so that I could move without the weight and pain on my muscles, joints, and bones. She brought humor and laughter to every situation. My family believed me and saw the physical evidence and never gave up.

My treatment journey was not easy, but I am here today in full remission, still with scars but with another amazing perspective that was bestowed on me at the age of sixteen. That *life is precious* perspective and perseverance makes all the complications of work and life seem minute. It makes all the fuss of the world pale in comparison. It teaches you to make a daily choice on mental attitude, what you should let bother you and what you should let go of. It makes you look at the pettiness of the world and laugh.

Perspective lessons continued to follow me throughout life. In an interview, I mentioned that I had lived a full life of perspective lessons in just about half of my life. I call all of these experiences perspective lessons because after getting through them, I could see so clearly that there was something deeper happening than what I could see on the surface. Things looked one way going in, but after coming out on the other side, I had a whole new perspective and sense of gratitude for whatever the situation taught me.

My dad's perspective and approach to his ALS diagnosis was extremely brave and inspiring and was yet another lesson on perspective I received. My mom was brave and resilient enough to care for him in their home. They modeled a GSD Factor mentality. He, my mom, my sister, and our family made it our mission to raise awareness, support, advocate, bring about change in research, and progress innovation for treatments as much as Dad was physically able to handle. He signed up for all the trials, from both western and eastern medicine. He was given a timer, not an exact timer, but more of a timer than most have. His perspective changed in those two years in that he wanted to share his story as a way to inspire and bring hope to others.

At the age of thirty-two, I lost my dad. He passed away four days after finding out that he was to be a first-time grandpa to my daughter. Nothing prepares you for losing a parent, especially losing at such a young age on the verge of them becoming a grandparent. Death is a natural part of life. We are all going to leave this earth one day. I think those, like my father, who are faced with a terminal diagnosis and subsequent timeline have a more urgent choice on how to impact the world before they leave. Do they go big and bold by sharing their story with the world? Do they go introspective and handle things on the home front, with friends and family, or worse, do they live in denial until the end? My dad chose the big and bold path, but in his final days, shared that he wished he had balanced that with the introspective a little better. I had another family member pass away who, unfortunately, took the denial path. Out of all three paths, that was definitely the hardest to witness. We wanted to enjoy moments and make memories, but they simply weren't there mentally. Even when given a timeline, be sure that your perspective is on the right trajectory with the right balance.

A short time after my daughter was born, I went back to work for a company that required weekly commuting. On this particular week's drive from the airport to my office, I was involved in a massive twelve-car accident that closed down a freeway for hours. Someone was texting while driving five lanes over from me. That person rear ended the person in front, which sent a domino effect of cars moving like ping pong balls across five lanes of morning traffic headed into downtown Nashville. Cars were flipping into ditches; it was a mess. As I saw the incident unfold before my eyes in slow motion, it felt like I was in a nightmare. I saw out of the corner of my right eye, a car being shot in my direction, and it was heading straight for the concrete median and a head-on-collision with me. I braced for impact but knew that if I stayed the course I could T-bone them and reduce their collision impact. I started praying to God, my angels, the Saints and to my heavenly family members to protect me. After impact and spinning in half a dozen donuts, I came to a screeching halt. I was fortunate enough to walk away from that traumatic event but not without physical bruises and, certainly, mental bruises. What I later learned from the emergency services is that my split-second decision to continue in my path of hitting that car actually saved the life of those occupants.

This accident happening so early on in my motherhood journey brought me a new perspective and a new weight of responsibility that I hadn't felt before. With my life flashing and spinning before my eyes, I wanted so badly to see my daughter and husband again. I wanted to hold them and not let go. It brought the perspective that life is precious, and we must hold on and treasure when we can, while we can. Sometimes in our lives we have to surrender because it is out of our control. It took great perseverance to get back into the car after that. It took great perseverance to drive past my accident spot, and even to this day when I drive past, I have to take some long breaths and say prayers of gratitude.

Perspective lessons at any young age shape you, mold you. I had a friend whose daughter was a cancer survivor at the age of three. He always talked about how that journey changed his and his family's perspectives on priorities, on family life, on work, and on friends forever.

My perspective has helped me in a professional setting too. Our ability to see true relevance in our professional or personal lives depends on our own history and experiences. Maybe life gave us perspective earlier than others. Maybe our experiences have caused our perspectives to be more raw, more authentic, more blunt. Many times, in our professional lives, the world and the people inside that world believe that everything is a fire and that it's life altering if we don't get that API to work or that email to go out. Thankfully, those of us with perspective can gently remind our colleagues that we aren't saving lives here. That email newsletter will be just as impactful the next hour as it was going to be in the originally scheduled hour.

I can recall a client that sent an aggressive timeline to transform a global technology across eighteen countries, and the project wasn't going according to plans. Emotions were running high that day, and everyone was running around with hair on fire because applications, integrations, and data weren't going to be done on time. Now, as you can imagine, as a consultant with a life of perspective, I often smile and remind everyone to take a breath and to go with the flow in situations like this. This particular day was no different. In an attempt to bring peace and perspective, I gently reminded the team that we weren't saving lives. We were replacing automobile parts. We weren't performing brain surgery. We were integrating System A to System B. At that exact moment, my sister, an ORC (Organ Recovery Coordinator) who manages the organ donation process, sent me an abstract picture of her walking down the hall. She explained that she had just walked a liver to a transporter so it could be airlifted to save a life. A hero had donated so that others could live. I shared this abstract image and story with those in the meeting that day. A hush fell across the meeting. You could have heard a pin drop. It gave me a chance to bring perspective to the situation. It was a necessary reminder to the team that although our work is important, it doesn't mean that we need to be unkind in our words to our colleagues or vendors. It doesn't mean that we need to ask our teams to sacrifice mental and physical well-being to get an application operational.

To those of you who are, perhaps, on a journey that resonates with any of these stories, I see you. I hear you. I'm cheering you on. Your GSD community is cheering you on. Your ability to be resilient is directly related to how you see the struggles and challenges you may face. I challenge you to consider the concept of perspective lessons the next time you find yourself in a difficult situation. It may be hard, but think about how much wiser you are going to be on the other side. Don't let it rattle you. You've got this.

GSD moment of reflection

Answer these prompts in the space below or on the GSD Factor Hub:

What relationships are enhancing and challenging your life in a good way to bring about growth?

_____

_____

_____

What is your greatest perspective lesson you have learned?

_____

_____

_____

What story of perseverance and perspective shaped you the most?

_____

_____

_____

www.gsdfactor.com

A SPACE TO DREAM BIG . . .

ACTION PLAN

FOR BUILDING RESILIENCE

Living out the resilient life takes sheer will. It requires grit. It requires you to dig deep. Resilience is the stamina and perseverance to acknowledge that life can be shitty sometimes, while also leaving room to acknowledge the moments for learning and growth. Many times, people will ask me for advice on how to be resilient. It's no simple process, but in attempting to reduce resilience to a series of actionable items, I suggest several things:

- Take time to grieve. You are a human, not a robot. Sometimes you need to get that raw emotion out, so that you can act out of logic and reason instead of repressed emotion.

- Keep a level-headed mindset, one that is open to seeing your situation from a different perspective. Remember those perspective lessons, and try to remain aware that whatever the situation is, there may be another way to look at it and learn.

- Ensure that as you experience hardship, you remain present in body, mind, soul, and emotion. No matter what hardships you are experiencing, you can still experience joy and the fullness of life and love in those challenging times as well, as long as you stay present and open to it.

- Trust the timing. You can do all that you can to manage your time and prepare for life, but there is no way to predict the many different obstacles life may present. Once something unexpected occurs, trust the timing and adjust as needed.

- When all seems to be failing or breaking, return to the basics. Return to simple mathematics because 1+1 will always be 2. Once you have regained your footing, you can begin to climb again. In short, this step can be summed up with the three Rs: Rest, Recharge and Retrospect. If you can't remember anything else about being resilient, doing those three things will keep you in a constant state of resilience.

After completing all of those steps, be sure to maintain your perspective by walking with humility and gratitude. Think about what you will be able to share with others at the end of this journey and be grateful that you made it to the other side to be able to share the wisdom you've gained. Think about how this weaves itself into your story. You are extraordinary. You are resilient. You are destined for great things.

Visit www.gsdfactor.com to join our GSD Factor Hub where you can take the Be Resilient assessment that will provide prescriptive recommendations based on where you want to ignite resilience in your life.

ATTRIBUTE SIX

BE **INFLUENTIAL**

The capability to lead by example as an actionable leader and connecting with those around you; you look to the future and also bring along the next generation alongside you and mentor them so they can stand on your shoulders.

"

The ultimate measure of a man is not where he stands in moments of comfort, but where he stands at times of challenge and controversy.

—Martin Luther King Jr.

"

LEADER BY EXAMPLE

What does being a leader mean to you? Is being a leader being someone who arrives early, stays late, and is always available with an open-door policy? Perhaps it's guiding the organization through unprecedented times. Is a leader someone who, despite many offerings of refuge, remains behind with his/her people? Is a leader someone who speaks of taking responsibility and actually does? Is a leader someone who roots for the underdog, supports the employee through a personal crisis, or simply shows up?

There are countless examples of leadership all around us: good leaders, bad leaders, young leaders, old leaders, leaders who were wise beyond their years, leaders who had so much experience that it almost crippled them, leaders who stood on the shoulders of their ancestors and led nations to victories, and leaders who made the ultimate sacrifice because it was more important for their people to see that they stood and fell instead of running away.

To me, being a leader is about knowing when to listen and when to act. It's about showing up. GSD Factor leaders are present, authentic leaders. They are GSD Factor leaders because they know when they need to lead, when to follow, when to push, and when to support.

Organizations have varying levels of leaders – inspirational leaders; visionary leaders; and imaginative, innovative solutionist leaders. All three are important, and the type of leader determines the culture of the company/organization. Inspirational leaders lead through motivation and appeal to the humanity of their teams. Fawn Weaver, CEO of Uncle Nearest Premium Whiskey is a great example of an inspirational leader. She's implemented many initiatives that show she is a leader who cares about people and bettering humanity. For example, she created the Nearest Green Foundation, which is a non-profit organization that provides scholarships to any descendant of Nearest Green. Gestures like that show that it's possible to be successful in business and dedicated to creating positive change in the world. Who wouldn't be inspired by a CEO like that?

Visionary leaders are those who can easily see how to take a company from level to level and into the future. They're always looking for the opportunity to take a calculated risk and watch it pay off. Robert (Bob) Iger fits that description perfectly. He had the foresight to execute the Disney-Pixar merger while he served as CEO of the entertainment giant. This merger was one of four major acquisitions made by Iger during his twenty-year stint as CEO of the company and contributed to a 404% increase in net income while he was there. Only a true visionary could produce that kind of profit increase, and that's exactly who Bob Iger is.

Finally, we have innovative solutionist leaders. They are the drivers of change. They aim to be the first and break the mold. People like Steve Jobs and Mark Benioff, CEO and Co-Founder of Salesforce. Since its inception in 1999, Benioff has helped drive the path of innovation and development at Salesforce making it the number one provider of customer relationship management software in the world! Leaders like Benioff specialize in building the impossible and changing entire systems. Organizations need people like that to find solutions and create new, better processes.

Some leaders are called in to solve and fix specific problems. They might also be needed to mediate a particular situation or to turn an organization around and save it from its downfall. No matter what kind of leader you are, one thing remains. Being a leader is hard.

My leadership style can be best described as a hybrid of all three. I'm an inspirational leader who can vision cast for others in a way that inspires them to be innovative solutionists. I know that's a mouthful, but it's true. I have a knack for finding people who have the drive and ambition to do a thing. They just need the inspiration and vision to get there. That's where I come in. I lead in such a way that those under my authority can see what it looks like to be confident, inquisitive, imaginative, resilient, present, and influential. Hopefully, the way I carry myself is an inspiration to them to see that they too can overcome great obstacles and still get shit done.

I've had plenty of opportunities to inspire others through my leadership. One especially painful time is the night my professional dance career ended for good. The years after my battle with Lyme's disease were proving hopeful for my recovery and return to dance. This was when I co-founded the dance school and began choreographing routines for my students and a couple of dance troupes. In addition to creating the choreography, I would often perform with the dance troupes. At one particular away performance, my troupe and I were performing to a popular song, "I Can Only Imagine" by Mercy Me. At the beginning of the first pre-chorus, I did a jump that I had done a thousand times before. However, something must have been different this time because as I came down, I felt one of the most painful feelings I would ever have in my knee. I didn't know exactly what happened, but I knew it was bad. At that moment, I thought I had two choices: crawl off stage in pain, which would essentially scare all of my students and the 300 plus kids in the audience or bear the pain and keep going. If you haven't figured it out yet, I chose the latter. I danced for three more minutes. By the time we were done, I was dragging my leg, and I kept dragging it right off stage into my father's arms. He had come into town as a surprise to support me. He would later tell me that he saw it happen and wondered why I kept going. My answer to him, the doctors, and everyone else who would ever ask was that I did not want to scare any of my students or the audience. We were performing for hundreds of children that day, and I thought the sight and sounds of my pain might scar them in a way that was traumatic and damaging. My choice had consequences, though. Those three minutes that I kept dancing on that injured knee and leg caused so much damage that the doctor had to postpone surgery for six weeks to allow the swelling time to subside. Six surgeries followed over six years, and my dance career was officially over. My doctor once asked me if it was worth it to keep dancing. My answer: Yes, because I didn't let my students and those children see their leader fall. That was important to me.

To this day, that's one thing they remember about me. That's the kind of leadership I want associated with me. I'm there with my team, motivating, pushing, and working with them. I need to also add that even though I never danced professionally again, I didn't stop teaching them. I taught from my wheelchair. I choreographed with the help of my sister. I haven't had instances of leadership that were as life-altering and drastic as this particular example since then, but the resilience that continued to develop in me as a result of that experience has served me well in other leadership positions.

The bottom line, friends, is that leadership comes with great responsibility and great pressure. If you are a family leader, you will have to make tough decisions about finances, health and the overall well-being of your family unit. If you are a leader in your company, you will probably have to make decisions that affect other people's abilities to lead their families. Countless lives are relying on your every decision. Your every move is under a microscope. It is nothing to take lightly.

Being a leader can also be lonely at times. I've often felt lonely as a leader, especially when I have to make tough decisions about finances or staffing. In those times, I relied heavily on my Insiders Board. I go to them first to get sound professional advice concerning the best overall picture for the company. I, then, check in with my Clan, to make sure that I'm approaching situations in the most compassionate and humane way as possible, given the circumstances. Leaders often face pivotal moments like these that may cause lives to change or be impacted positively and/or negatively. You have to be comfortable with the uncomfortable. If you are a leader, you are at the helm of change. You have to be good with change. You are driving change. You have a say, even when no one else sees it, because you're the leader. The buck stops with you.

Rachel Hollis, author of *Girl, Stop Apologizing*, once said, "I believe we can change the world. But first, we've got to stop living in fear of being judged for who we are." A leader can't live in fear. He/ she can't worry about what people will say. They have to be confident enough in the change they are bringing, confident in themselves, in their beliefs, in their decisions.

Being a leader calls for a level of courage like no other. It's saying I'm going to stand in as tribute for my team when there is a scapegoat hunt afoot. It's the courage to go in front of a firing squad and answer each and every question without emotion, just facts. In a merger and acquisition situation, it's saying let my team keep their jobs and roll into the new organization and I'll step away.

For those who are aspiring to be leaders, we need you. We need good leaders. We need leaders who walk with authentic conviction, who actively listen, who have empathy. We need leaders who know when and how to take action, who can encourage and empower, who seek equality across their organizations, beyond race, gender, and sexuality. We need leaders who give back to their communities. We need leaders who are thinking about the next generation and preparing those future leaders to stand on their predecessors' shoulders. Remember, leadership is not for the faint of heart. It has its challenges, but it is also so rewarding.

The biggest lessons that I've learned from being a leader is conviction and confidence in my decisions and my willingness to exhibit humility. When I make a decision, I do so unapologetically. Once, I had to hold a seasoned employee accountable for her lack of progress on our team. I had conversations with her and let her know the ways in which we all were making efforts to increase our productivity and performance. I tried to work with her, and I made every option available for her to improve. Unfortunately, she was set in her ways and had no desire to adjust. I did not change my expectations, though. Consequently, she resigned. I knew that I could not budge because that would show the team that my expectations had exceptions, which they did not. As a result, other members of the team recognized that my standards were set. People either began to meet them, or they left. The end result, however, was a better, more well-rounded and productive team that was birthed out of my decision not to budge with my expectations for that one seasoned employee.

When I say no, it's a full sentence, and I do so without apology. However, I'm willing to acknowledge when I have made a mistake or something has gone awry. I'm a human, and therefore, not impervious to making mistakes. One mistake I made actually involved not terminating someone's employment sooner. This particular person was underperforming and full of negativity. After having a few conversations, they let me know that they really needed the job and would improve. To my disappointment, they did not improve. As a matter of fact, they actually got worse and impacted the entire team. That was a mistake, and I admit and accept that. I don't blindly stand by my decisions, I'm aware of them and the impact they will have. I maintain a willingness to be teachable and to learn from my mistakes.

When I make a decision that's not popular, I stand by it and defend it with a good counter-argument. Similar to the decisions I mentioned earlier, this unpopular decision surrounded the resignation of one of the most-liked employees on the team. Everybody loved to have her around, but this person was toxic in that she loved gossip and continued to do improper, unprofessional things that most of the team was unaware of. Upon her departure, there was a mixture of shock and confusion as to why she left. I allowed her to have her dignity through resignation rather than termination. People questioned me, and rather than tarnishing her reputation, I would just reply that I understood that everybody was not happy with her decision to resign. There was no need for me to disclose what she was doing because my goal was not to harm her, only to help her reach her potential. Her decision to do so, or in her case, not to do so while at that particular company was completely up to her.

My goal as a leader has always been to stand up and protect those under me; I was their advocate. I made sure to show up for my team. I showed up on the 3AM calls, even when I couldn't really do anything to help with an IT release. I jumped on just so they would know I was there with them. I showed up, and that was enough. Sometimes, all they need to know is that you care and that you see them as more than just a means to profit. It's the same support we talk about with the GSD Factor attribute of being present. At times, your presence is all that is needed for those in your circle to know that they can trust and depend on you. That's all a part of leading by example. I cannot ask my team to do anything that I'm not at least willing to show up for.

When those personal crises happen to someone on the team, good leaders are there listening and saying, "We've got you. Don't worry about work. Focus on your family." These are the times when it's best to take off your boss hat, and put on your good human hat. I had the opportunity to do just that when one of my team members came to me and informed me that she was embarking on her motherhood journey. It wasn't the traditional route, and she faced several struggles during the process of getting pregnant and during her entire pregnancy. I hadn't yet become a mother, but it was important for me to show her and the rest of the company how important it is to support employees as they choose the path of parenthood. Throughout her journey, I made sure that we gave her the flexibility she needed to get to appointments and provide support in whatever capacity necessary. She still had to work, but we developed her own maternity plan that allowed her to still be productive and take care of herself and her child as well. At the end of the day, family rules and that's all that matters. In those moments, that's all that an employee, contractor, or vendor needs to hear. You will create fierce loyalty, and when you need them to show up for that big deliverable or turning the impossible to possible, your team will deliver. Why? Because you showed up for them time and time again, even when it wasn't work related.

Although leadership has many tough challenges, it has sweet moments too. Those moments when I can support a team member, their family, or a nonprofit organization that means something to them are invaluable. When my team has brought charities and organizations to the forefront to see how we can support them and give back, we make it a point to show up. We give to them monetarily, as well as in time and resources. By giving to that team member's family or nonprofit organization, that team member by extension feels as if they have been given a gift. There are moments when I can coach a team member through personal struggles and encourage them not to give up on themselves. Letting them know that the team will not give up on them, and seeing those members turn their lives around or excel in their next opportunity is hugely rewarding.

When one of my team members came to me with news that she was diagnosed with Leukemia, I cried with her; we embraced, and then we got busy making sure she was taken care of. We scheduled a meal train for her. We planned for her surgeries by adjusting her hours and making sure that another co-worker with whom she was close also had flexibility to support her and attend appointments and treatments with her. The company even became a corporate sponsor for the Leukemia Lymphoma Society. I left that company many years ago, but that team member and I still have a friendship to this day because of the bonds we created during our time working together. Opportunities like this present themselves fairly often when you're in leadership. You can't always do as much as we did in my situation, but in moments like these, it's important to exercise compassion and allow your humanity to flourish.

Being a leader is also having the boldness to hold other leaders in your sphere of influence accountable. I once had a client whose key stakeholder was a massive bully. The only way they knew how to communicate was to curse and yell at their team members. I confronted this leader and shared how ineffective this communication method was. I demonstrated to them a different way of approaching, communicating, and, ultimately, delivering ahead of schedule with a happy team. This client had never been coached or mentored correctly. They had been taught that the only way to be effective was to bully people into submission. They would bark orders with crazy deliverable timelines and then go home to their family. It took time, but I was able to coach a transformation in that leader by letting them know and demonstrating what effective leadership should look like, by reflecting their comments and actions back to them. I would repeat what they said and make them aware of how it could be perceived, and then we would find better ways to tailor their message or action to fit their intended audience. Leading by example might require you to have to put those skills to the test, even among your peers, but don't avoid it because that's another way to inspire or motivate your team.

Being a leader, at times, calls for pushing your team to excellence or raising them to the next level of growth. Some misunderstand this pushing as a way to bully or yell, but that does nothing to motivate the team in the long run. Sure, they may complete the initial project, but you will have lost them mentally, if not permanently. Effective leadership means pushing your team, rolling up your sleeves and saying, "What can I do to help?" Many leaders in the IT space often start off as administrators, architects, or even developers. Oftentimes, those leaders of their organizations let you know who is CEO or COO because title is important to them. I once had a situation where I experienced the exact opposite. I was a customer needing some immediate help on a project where failure was not an option, and we had to hit a deadline for a regulatory time period. I was introduced to one organization in particular, and I was immediately impressed with the team that was there, listening, rolling up their sleeves, developing, building and springing into action. I later found out that the solution architect on my project was actually the company's CTO, and the developer was the CEO! This company is a global organization with over two thousand employees, yet at that moment, title and role didn't matter. They were there to GSD because they knew FINAO (Failure Is Not An Option).

Even if it's a little bit of help, if it's guiding the conversation, or just being present with the team as they fix it or solve a problem, your willingness to help will be appreciated. Your presence as a leader speaks more volume than you know. Perhaps it's having the humility to know that you can't deliver to a level of excellence that is your standard, or the project is too big for your organization. Being a leader is also standing your ground when in contract negotiations by saying, "This is our value. This is our worth." This concept also applies to your personal career decisions. Being a courageous leader in your professional journey might require you to decline the initial offer, counter with what you believe to be your worth and be willing to walk away if they don't accept. That's walking out courageous actionable leadership.

What about you? Are you a GSD leader? Do you want to improve your leadership? Perhaps you weren't mentored well. That's fine. It's not too late. Do you want to transform your leadership skills? You've already taken the first step by showing up, by reading or listening to this book. Now let's make you an effective GSD Factor actionable leader.

GSD moment of reflection

Answer these prompts in the space below or on the GSD Factor Hub:

What does leadership mean to you?

_____

_____

_____

What kind of a leader are you?

_____

_____

_____

What kind of lessons or mentorship were you raised with?

_____

_____

_____

www.gsdfactor.com

A SPACE TO DREAM BIG . . .

A SPACE TO DREAM BIG . . .

21

CHALLENGING THE STEREOTYPES

As you can imagine with the name of my book and company, I don't mind using the word *shit*. Countless times I've encountered individuals, both men and women, who either love that I feel confident enough to use it, or they are appalled. I have a sign in my office that is visible on my camera, and it says, "Team Get Shit Done." I love that picture. If my prospect or candidate is offended by that sign, then it's a quick way to gauge if they will be a good fit for me, my team, and my organization. That sign, or random expletive, is a precursor to my leadership style and influence. If they can't work with that, they probably can't work with me.

I know I don't fit the mold of what is expected of women leaders. When I started in the corporate world, women were still being held to standards based on antiquated stereotypes and societal gender roles. We were expected to be demure and soft-spoken, so loud, brash and opinionated Misha, obviously, rubbed some people the wrong way. Many deals and business partnerships were created over golf games, drinks, and football talk, all things from which women were largely excluded. Wouldn't you know that my dad, being the visionary that he was, made sure I learned to play golf and talk football before I got into this business so that I would be able to hold my own in those situations. Of course, it paid off.

I remember once (maybe twice) having to not-so-subtly inform a co-worker of my football pedigree after he made a snide remark implying that I didn't know anything about the game because I was a girl. He got a quick history of the Bleymaier football dynasty, including my dad's two-time Rose Bowl wins, my uncles playing for Air Force Academy and UCLA and, of course, my Uncle Gene Bleymaier's pioneering athletic director career at Boise State University, including the blue field and now Bleymaier Football Center. I don't like to name-drop, but, hey, sometimes we've got to use our voices, right? That coworker, like many people over the years, quickly found out that I was different. I don't believe in stereotypes, and I definitely don't fit them. Yes, I am a woman, but my gender will not determine how I lead or how others will treat me as a leader. I am a capable, efficient leader, who happens to be a woman. That is all.

My get shit done attitude and signs give insight into my personality and the way I view life. The fact that I use an expletive has nothing to do with the quality of my work. It's just another way for me to use my voice. To me, being a woman in leadership means that in some industries, we are trailblazers; it means that sometimes we are the only woman in the room. In other instances, it means that we are the first at something. Sometimes it means that we are breaking glass ceilings. Many times, we are scrutinized a little more than our male counterparts. As a result, being a woman in leadership can come with a great deal of pressure in addition to the built-in pressures of leadership in general. That's why we need even more women leaders because the ones we have don't need to feel like the outliers. Of course, our standards for excellence and success should be high, but that should be the case for all leaders, regardless of gender. No woman should have to feel like she is grateful to just be at the table, because she has a right to that table just like her male counterparts. She also shouldn't be made to feel that in the event that she makes a mistake (and she will because, well…human), she has ruined anything for her female successors because being in leadership doesn't make one perfect. That should be the overall ideology of all leaders.

In my experience as a woman, and in listening to other women, one of the hardest things for women, in business, especially, is believing that we are worthy to have it all. Well, let me tell you, unequivocally, without a shadow of a doubt, we are worthy. As a matter of fact, let's just dispel the myth of having to choose. We can have fulfilling professions. We can have our spouses. We can also be mothers. We don't have to choose because men don't have to choose. No one has to choose.

At times, I also think people hold several incorrect assumptions about women in leadership. Some assume that she must work to contribute to the home. Some assume that she is a wife, mom, and employee. Some assume that if she is not a mom, it's because she chose career over motherhood. Some assume that if she is not a wife, it's because she chose career over marriage, or the marriage failed because of work. It is still a novelty to some that women can be so many things, and there does not have to be a reason. The blanket assumptions that are laid out for women don't apply to every woman, and let us be honest, it's really no one's business anyway.

Oftentimes, women get a certain, usually negative, label or stereotype because of how the world views them. Here are some of my own life examples. In the past, I have been in situations where I disagreed with a statement or action, and I raised my voice or showed passion. Sometimes, I argued with a male counterpart, which is normal. People don't always agree on everything. However, in those instances, I was inaccurately tagged or labeled as being "spun up," highly emotional, overly passionate, or "flying hot." My male counterparts, however, were not perceived or labeled in the same way. They were not seen as highly passionate. They were not seen as being "spun up." They were just seen as being them.

This same problematic practice of attaching negative labels to women as a result of their passion and emotion can also be detrimental to men, but in different ways. We often see men being advised to lead with logic and avoid emotional decisions or expression for fear of being irrational. That's not always good advice, though. It is important for the male population to know that it is okay for a man to be passionate, emotional, or to have strong convictions about some things.

I recently worked with an architect, who was Italian and highly passionate about his viewpoint and how he liked to create and approach his designs. Almost everybody on the team suggested that his feelings and actions were just because he is Italian. In this day and age, where we come from and our cultural backgrounds should not have negative connotations attached to them, especially not in a professional setting. Our cultural differences should not matter for male or female, but I think if he had been a female, people would not have associated his passion with his nationality. They would have just said, "Oh, she is a woman, and she's just being a protective non-collaborating witch." Let us be honest, raw and authentic, right here and right now. All of us have been there and witnessed it, and neither situation is fair or professional.

I do not think that it is fair to assume that their actions or emotions are simply a result of their genders. Should a person's cultural differences and approaches to life be taken into consideration and respected when conducting business on a global scale? Absolutely – 100%, but I do not think that people should be assigned some kind of cultural label because of an emotional reaction.

Being a woman in leadership means that somebody has fought the fight and has embraced the GSD Factor mindset. Somebody has determined that failure is not an option. Somebody has embodied the practice of failing quickly and trying again. Being a woman in leadership means embracing the life cycle of launch, pause, pivot, and relaunch. I think that when you see a woman in leadership you see someone that has had to overcome stereotypes on top of everyday obstacles, somebody that has to work a little harder. You see a woman who is the personification of resilience.

I share these viewpoints with you both as a woman and as a leader, but I want to challenge all of us, both male and female across all races, religions, cultures, and identity expressions. There are differences, but we should be able to come together and just be professionals. Let us be good humans, and let us band together and use our specific influences to make sure that we are taking care of one another. Let's make sure we are respecting each other's views and supporting one another even when we do not agree. It's okay to disagree, and it is okay to voice those grievances. Disagreements should not automatically result in negative stereotypes. Disagreements should not prevent collaboration. If anything, disagreements should foster respect.

I would much rather, as a leader in the insurance and technology industry and as an entrepreneur and founder of multiple companies, have people on my team that step out to present different perspectives. Leadership should be open and available for all people in all industries, and when that happens, it's good for everyone. Be wary of stereotypes. They bring little benefit to any company or organization because they usually perpetuate negativity over positivity and conformity over uniqueness and diversity. If all your leaders look and act the same, then your organization will as well. Diversity in leadership, however, leads to diversity in employee makeup, which leads to a more balanced, well-rounded company that knows how to GSD, and who wouldn't want that? GSD leaders understand how powerful having influence is and that we can affect change in all industries where women and other minorities are underrepresented in both leadership and general positions by challenging all the negative stereotypes that may have prevented women from upward mobility. What do you say? Are you up for the challenge?

GSD moment of reflection

Answer these prompts in the space below or on the GSD Factor Hub:

Have you ever been misunderstood because of a stereotype or generalization?

_____

_____

Have you ever felt reduced to one aspect of your identity?

_____

_____

What's a way that you can advocate for yourself?

_____

_____

Is there a group or individual or organization that you can advocate for?

_____

_____

www.gsdfactor.com

A SPACE TO DREAM BIG . . .

A SPACE TO DREAM BIG . . .

HEROES + SHEROES + MENTORS

This chapter is about showing gratitude and thanks. It's about my heroes and mentors, those that have inspired me. These are the people that have impacted my life, people that saw something in me when I didn't and called something forth inside of me.

The first person I want to thank is someone I call my warrior princess, who I'll also refer to as WP. WP and I met on an airplane from Chicago to Nashville. The way she tells our first encounter, I was this girl who bounced up with a head of curls and smiles and boldly asked if I could share the power plug before we boarded the plane. We started talking at that moment and didn't stop until we reached the Nashville airport parking lot.

Her energy was amazing. We found an immediate synergy – a sisterly bond in empowering women of our varying generations. Our visions and our dreams were aligned. She was what some might call a jack of all trades. She was an artist, musician, entrepreneur, mentor, and leader who had a heart for investing in her community, specifically into other African American women. This woman was into everything. She owned a production company, restaurant, even a shopping center. Yes, she bought an abandoned shopping center and began setting up offices there for her many business ventures with plans to bring more jobs to the community to help empower those within her sphere of influence. To put it lightly, she was a powerhouse. It was like she saw no limits. She dreamed even bigger than I do, and that's saying a lot!

It may not look like it on paper, but my WP and I had many things in common, especially our desire to empower, motivate, and support women. That was the bond that connected us and sparked our short partnership. When I met her, I was still working in the corporate sector, but I felt like something was missing and that there was more purpose for me with regards to helping others. All of my experiences as a woman in corporate America showed me that women really needed and wanted encouragement and support in their professional and personal lives. I wanted to find ways to help people, women, specifically to find success in every part of their lives, and so did my WP. We wanted to give women a voice, to equip them with tools to improve their personal and professional lives. We talked about dreams of inspiring the next generation. Her desire was to be a trailblazer in the black community in Alabama, and she wanted me to come alongside her and share that mission and display that power of reconciliation across age, race, and backgrounds.

So many times women give to others but forget to care for themselves, so we wanted to start by teaching women to care for themselves. We actually co-hosted an event in her hometown that was our first step towards building this community of empowered women. The event focused on health and wellness, which was a passion of mine at the time. We then moved to equipping and empowering women with their best wardrobes. WP's daughter owned a boutique, so she covered this part, and let's be clear, it wasn't just about what you put on your body, it was all about how you wore it, how you walked, your posture, your stance. It was tall and loud and proud, and the wardrobe had to have a lot of color! Finally, WP covered spiritual and emotional health, and we all contributed to the conversation around career, destiny, and purpose. It was a great kick-off to what we envisioned as a long-lasting partnership.

After this event, WP and I began planning our future collaborations. The next big goal was to help women in their careers. She and I would use our combined knowledge and experience to give advice and resources to help women navigate their professional journeys. WP was an entrepreneur and was accustomed to dreaming big. She wanted to share that love for vision and goal-casting with those around her. She wanted to plant the seeds of those dreams into other women, water them, and help them grow. That's part of what made her so inspirational. This was her destiny. It was obvious from the support she received by women attending that first event we hosted that the community trusted and embraced her wisdom and care. This was walking out the fullness of the purpose she believed God had called her to. She was strong and beautiful and great.

The last time I spoke to my warrior princess, we had one of our crazy, fast dream-big sessions where we just threw a bunch of ideas out there and saw the synergies unfolding as she shared what God had been showing her. I was actually sitting in the pick-up line at my daughter's school talking to WP on the phone. There was nothing strange in her voice. She didn't mention any health problems. We were just doing our usual vision-casting and dreaming big. We were making plans for our next event, and before the conversation finished, she took some time to motivate and inspire me. She was the encouragement I needed at the time when I was trying to figure out my next step; she spoke into my life. She saw things that I didn't see in myself. She often told me how she loved being a warrior and how she lived out her warrior spirit daily. That was in January. My warrior princess transitioned to the next life a month later. It was sudden and unexplainable, but her passing left a great void in my life and the community she loved. I only knew her for a few, short years, and the effects she had on me were great.

It was my interaction with her that lit the spark of GSD in my life. All the dream-big sessions we had gave me the motivation to start this journey. In a way, her legacy will live on through me, but more importantly, her legacy will live on through the community that she spent so much time pouring into. She was the living embodiment of the GSD Factor life.

My next great mentor is my Fairy Godmother, FG for short. FG helped my career trajectory and was a critical piece to my transition from a small business into the corporate world. She was a trailblazing recruiter in the Nashville area and was one of the founding members of a staffing company that went on to gain national renown. She redefined how you recruit someone but also how questions:

STATE the situation.

List out the TASKS.

Explain the ACTION items.

Share the RESULTS.

Then she became my advocate. FG was like my walking cover letter, my agent. She was known to call up companies and say, "You have to interview this girl. Hear her passion, her motivation, her domination. Just have a conversation with her, and you will be glad that you did." Most companies would say, "Sure, after we see her resume," but she would say, "No, not until you meet her." For those companies that she did get me interviews with, they would call her back up and say, "Damn, you were right. She is incredible." She had others say, "Oh, she's amazing, but our process and procedures won't possibly allow us to continue with the interview process or hire her because she doesn't have a degree."

Through it all, she persevered and got through to multiple companies over the course of my career, for which I'm forever grateful.

She went far beyond the job requirements of a recruiter. Before each interview, she would host me at her house where we would pick out my interview outfit, accessorize, practice walking and standing tall; then practice interview questions, similar to role play. Even in her retirement, she is still recruiting for me as my walking cover letter and sending people my way that I just need to meet.

She also taught me that networking and interactions with people matter. It's in part because of her that I have the ability to speak life and vision into people, helping them dream big for their lives. She taught me, in regard to potential employees, at least, to have a conversation. Never dismiss an email or direct message. She taught me that even though I may not see the immediate synergy with a candidate, or may not have a job for them, I should still have a conversation. It could impact my life and may impact their life. They could influence me, and I could influence them. That's a way for me to become part of the solution. It's a way for me to be that light, that sunshine for someone else. As an interviewer or a hiring manager, I may not choose that person, but for those few moments, we can make real connections. You never know where your worlds will intersect, so it's important to give every encounter a chance. You might meet that person again. It could be soon; it could be later. My FG believed in that, and she passed that ideology on to me. Countless people have come to me after interviews and said, "You didn't hire me, but what you said to me that day changed my life and career forever."

FG loves taking credit for my husband and me coming together because we met at work, the company where she placed me. She would constantly comment that if she hadn't placed me at that job, I would have never met my husband. Needless to say, she made sure she was in attendance at our company-wide engagement party. As an amazing woman leader in her community, continuing to fight her Parkinson's disease in retirement, she is a warrior. She has never let her physical challenges stop her. She's never let her physical limitations mean anything. She continues to push. She continues to live. She continues to be the power networker. She continues to fight.

Fairy Godmother is a GSD Factor woman. She embodies the GSD Factor mentorship mentality. She embodies the GSD mentor network. She saw a small girl that could have a big impact in this world. She saw the impossible. She saw somebody with potential and drive, and she made an investment in me. She showed up for me, and she didn't even know me. It was because of her I learned that there are so many men and women out there that need that mentor, need that coach, need that ONE person to advocate, speak up and SHOW up. If she had not shown up, how different would my life trajectory be? If she hadn't used her voice, maybe I wouldn't have landed in a company where I met my husband. She invested her wisdom, her time and her energy. She equipped me with the practical execution tools that I used then and continue to use for my career. She continues to inspire me and inspire others. There's not a week that goes by that I don't have a conversation with someone that shares their positive Fairy Godmother story.

One of my biggest lessons from her is that a person's resume on paper is just that. In some cases, you have to see beyond the paper; you have to see that person. At the least, see the interview as a way to mentor. Perhaps they may not be walking out their full destiny. They may not know what they want, but your interview or your coaching may be the catalyst for that person that will change the trajectory of their life.

Today, I still use the STAR methodology across everything – interviews, board meetings, investor reviews, sharing case studies, etc. I've even taught my daughter how to use it in her elementary school presentations. We should call it the Fairy Godmother Methodology.

GSD reader, I would like to challenge you with this. Have that conversation. Respond to that email or direct message. Talk to that kid in high school, as they are the next generation. Talk to that new college graduate that's looking at their career. You never know; a few minutes of your time may change the course of their life. Maybe you have that candidate in front of you today that doesn't have all the traditional credentials, but they have that passion, that fire in their belly. Give them a chance. Change the rules; change the guidelines. Make shit happen.

In addition to having my warrior princess and fairy godmother as mentors who were close enough for me to call and visit, I also have sheroes that I look up to who are not so close. I've mentioned other people who have inspired me throughout the book, but there's one more person whose story resonates with me in a more unique and powerful way. That person is Shania Twain. If you're not familiar with her, here's a short, far-from-all-inclusive biography.

Shania Twain is a Canadian born singer-songwriter who has sold over 100 million records and holds the title of "Queen of Country Pop." She paved the way for women in country music and many other genres with her boldness, confidence, and authenticity. Though she is one of the most decorated singers in music history, what's most impressive to me about Shania is not her musical ability. It's the way in which she embodies so many of the GSD Factor attributes. It was her ability to be confident in her talent as a songwriter and to be innovative with her fashion and creativity that helped land her in the top of the country music charts. She has shown resilience by pursuing her dreams after losing both her parents in a car accident and then becoming sole caretaker of her three younger siblings. Get this: she also showed resilience by continuing to sing after surviving Lyme's disease, open throat vocal surgery, and a messy divorce after an affair between her ex-husband and best friend! She is a text-book example of someone who is living the GSD Factor life out loud. Her life and career has inspired me and gives me a more recognizable example to point to when people ask me what the GSD Factor looks like.

Everybody needs a hero or mentor. Life can be challenging sometimes, and even the strongest, most successful people can benefit from having someone in their corner to motivate them and give them that extra push. Reflect on who those people have been in your life, and if they are still here with us, do your best to show your gratitude and honor them. While you're at it, ask yourself this question, "To whom have I been a hero or a mentor?" If you can't answer that question, I challenge you to make room in your life to pour into someone else, without expectation, simply as a way to return the gift of mentorship that was given to you. May we all continue to learn from our heroes and mentors, and may we live a life that is worthy of being someone else's. What a great way to get shit done!

GSD moment of reflection

Answer these prompts in the space below or on the GSD Factor Hub:

Who is your hero or mentor? Have you told them?

_____

_____

_____

Who can you mentor? How can you impact the next generation?

_____

_____

_____

What actionable leadership can you take that will break down barriers between gender, race, generation, and identity expression?

_____

_____

_____

www.gsdfactor.com

A SPACE TO DREAM BIG . . .

ACTION PLAN

FOR BEING INFLUENTIAL

Part of being a GSDer, of having the GSD Factor, is being a leader. To me, being a leader is about knowing when to listen and when to act. It's about showing up. GSD Factor leaders are present, authentic leaders. They are leaders because they know when they need to lead, when to follow, when to push, and when to support.

Leadership is not for the faint of heart. It can be lonely but rewarding. You lead by example, and while looking to the future, you also bring the next generation alongside you. You mentor them, so they can stand on your shoulders. You don't feel success until you can see your mentees trailblazing, breaking glass ceilings, and going beyond your wildest dream big for them.

As a leader and a GSDer, challenge injustice, give voice to the under-voiced, and stand for equality. While bringing along the next generation, honor those that have gone before you – your mentors, your heroes, and your sheroes. Thank them for paving the way.

The Teachers Insurance and Annuity Association (TIAA), has recently partnered with a new brand ambassador Abby Wambach, U.S. Women's soccer Hall-of-Famer for her U.S. and International career performances and impact on the sport, who, in retirement, has turned author and activist. They have launched a new campaign bringing awareness to retirement inequality for women entering retirement including research and statistics that show that even in 2022, women retire with 30% less income than men on average.

Now this is where they embody the GSD Factor attribute; they tie this to how they make an impact on future generations:

"There are some things you don't just do for you. You do them for the ones who come after you. Together, we can retire inequality for good." Yes to this! They are using their voice to change the here, the now, and for the ones who come next.

Identify what kind of leader you want to be or aspire to be and do that, live that. All three are important, and the type of leader determines the culture of the company/organization:

- Inspirational leaders lead through motivation and appeal to the humanity of their teams.

- Visionary leaders are those who can easily see how to take a company from level to level and into the future.

- Innovative solutionist leaders are the drivers of change. They aim to be the first and break the mold.

You may be one of these types of leaders or a hybrid, just find the one that speaks to your true authentic self, resonates courage, and above all *be who YOU are and get shit done*. That's it. It's that simple.

Visit www.gsdfactor.com to join our GSD Factor Hub where you can take the Be Influential assessment that will provide prescriptive recommendations based on where you want to ignite influence in your life.

THE GSD FACTOR LIFE

All of the attributes we've discussed in this book – being Confident, Inquisitive, Imaginative, Present, Resilient, and Influential – are all parts of the GSD Factor life. I hope you've gathered, by this point, that many of my lessons come from interactions with my tiny humans, my children. Recently, we were watching *Frozen 2*, and the song "Show Yourself" seemed to speak to me like never before. The whole premise of the song basically asserts that whatever it is that you are looking for to give you validation or permission to succeed can only be found in you. You are the answer to your questions. You are the one you have been waiting for. That's what I want you to take away from this book.

I can tell you what worked for me, the attributes that I've found to have encouraged and transformed me, but, ultimately, the action is your responsibility. It's not up to me, your Insiders Board, or your Clan to do the work. You have to do the work for yourself. You have to show up. You have to decide which tools you are adding to your toolbox.

Whether you hold a formal position of leadership in your career, family or organization, being a GSDer will cause others to look to you for guidance. It's inevitable, because once all these attributes are working in your life, people are going to notice that you get shit done. Then, they're going to start watching you and maybe even asking you how you do it. Here's the challenge for you. I have shared the wisdom and strategies that have helped me accomplish goals and experience success both professionally and personally. I know these attributes work. I am the evidence. What will you do with this knowledge? It's now up to you to decide how you use it. How do you apply these attributes to your life?

You may decide after reading this that you are good with where you are, and that's okay. However, I hope that after reading this, there is something inside you saying, "I want to get shit done." When that happens, know that you've got this. You are not alone. You have taken that first step to say, "I am here. Hear my voice. Know my name. Watch as I write history for the next generation. Witness my story, my journey."

Now, let's get shit done!

TO THOSE WHO HAVE
HELPED ME GSD

To my husband, my cheerleader, my best listener and the person who challenges me to think about life differently. I'm honored to walk this journey of life alongside you.

To my kids who are teaching me that being a Mom is the greatest gift and the hardest course I'll ever take. I've learned to listen to your mini life lessons, because even though I'm your Mom, you are still teaching me.

To my sister, someone who has lived out the GSD Factor life and walked alongside me every step of the way and who just gets it. Most times we don't even have to say what we are thinking because we already know, and our faces and eyebrows tell the story.

To my fellow "goddam Cheetah." To have a friend that runs through career, marriage, motherhood, and all the in between, who shows up and brings humor to the situation.

To my dad and mom, who taught me how to do things and how not to do things. Dad, you passed on the Bleymaier drive and passion about business, sharing the story, raising awareness and resources for those less fortunate, and staying positive even when life is halted. Mom, you passed on the importance of researching and knowing our story, changing our story, and sharing the story. Thank you both for the countless lessons.

To my teams who have grown up with me, lived with me learning my strategies, put up with my dream big sessions, tried and failed my theories, and still showed up. When I talk about my "Team GSD," you know who you are, and you will always be part of this GSD Factor story.

To my mentors who taught me what to do and what not to do; to the men and women that told me I wasn't educated enough, was too loud, was too type A for a girl, was too bossy; to those that said "DO. Do it your way, with your energy, with your voice, and I will support and encourage along the way;" I say thank you to those that were part of my darkest days because through you, I learned life's greatest lessons. They say we rise from the ashes. Thank you for burning the shit up. Because of you, I RISE, and my voice is now heard by many who will rise too!

To my "running editor." I couldn't have done this without you. Thank you for the countless hours of listening, writing, and reading alongside me. You have relived my 40-year life in the last 12 months and even still continue to show up.

To my God: I haven't always understood, but I trusted. I haven't always believed, but I hung on to your promises. Sometimes you showed me the path clearly, but sometimes you didn't. One thing is for sure, my life has been a tapestry of faith, love, and never losing hope.

RESOURCES

GSDers to watch out for:

- Antonio Javar Hairston, author of *The Center: How Our Thoughts, Feelings and Beliefs Shape our Destiny*
- Bob Iger, CEO of Disney
- Fawn Weaver, CEO of Uncle Nearest Premium Whiskey
- Lauren Ruth Martin, LPC-MHSP, podcast host of *9toKIND*
- Marc Benioff, chair and Co-CEO at Salesforce
- Melissa Unsell-Smith, host of *Catalytic Icon*
- Abby Wambach, soccer legend, speaker, activist, New York Times Best Selling Author

Companies to check out:

- Slumberkins
- Masterclass
- Mindtools

Search engines to fuel your research:

- Gender Equality Fund, a search engine for finding gender equality stats in the workplace
- Positive Words Research, a search engine for finding good, kind, inspirational words

Articles to inform and inspire:

- Forbes' *How Fawn Weaver Created Uncle Nearest Premium Whiskey From Hidden History*
- Exploding Topics' *74+ Shocking Women in Tech Statistics 2023*
- S&P Market Intelligence's *Female Insurance Leaders Work Against Odds to Open Doors for Other Women*
- Salesforce's *Salesforce and New Brand Partner and Advisor Matthew McConaughey Debut #TeamEarth Campaign, a Rallying Cry to Build a Better Future Together*

Printed in Great Britain
by Amazon